CARY GRANT

The next day, Archie went to Marathon Street to a Paramount Publix sound stage studio. He told himself to relax, to look at the camera, to act naturally. He remembered Casey Robinson's directions to keep his right side towards the camera and to keep his chin up to diminish the size of his neck. He was determined to do well.

When the test was ready for viewing, there was good news and bad news. The bad news was that Mrs Gering didn't impress a single one of the studio executives who watched. The good news was that Archie Leach looked great.

Archie was staying at San Simeon. Within a week, he got a call there from B.P. Schulberg. Paramount offered the young Englishman a contract for five years plus options and a salary of $450 per week. 'A standard deal,' Schulberg said. 'One other thing,' he added, 'if you accept, you'll have to change your name.'

CARY GRANT

**Chuck Ashman and
Pamela Trescott**

A STAR BOOK
published by
the Paperback Division of
W. H. Allen & Co. Plc

A Star Book
Published in 1988
by The Paperback Division of
W. H. Allen & Co. Plc
44 Hill Street, London W1X 8LB

First published in Great Britain by
W. H. Allen & Co. Plc in 1987

Copyright © Chuck Ashman and Pamela Trescott, 1986

Printed and bound in Great Britain by
Anchor Brendon Ltd, Tiptree, Essex

ISBN 0 352 32130 X

CONTENTS

CARY
GRANT

INTRODUCTION

IF THERE WERE AN effective way to poll the public and the press of all English-speaking countries, 83-year-old Cary Grant would still undoubtedly win any contest to be nominated the world's most charming man. But, unlike the handful of other swash-buckling romantics that might appear on such a list with the former Archibald Leach, Grant is also rightly credited with a natural flair for sophisticated comedy. He has kept audiences laughing as well as fantasizing for decades.

The debonair, sexy style of the film world's leading leading man has attracted the full gamut of appreciative women, from Mae West to Sophia Loren. It even affects the office workers at film studios and Fabergé's corporate offices in New York. More than one secretary will readily admit to the unprecedented excitement when Cary arrived, smiled or gave his autograph. Grant is not the only elderly former movie idol who seems to have got better . . . not just older. But he is certainly the leader of the pack.

During a recent lecture tour, Grant was confronted by one cocky young female reporter who thought the actor's mysti-que was grossly exaggerated. She bragged to her colleagues that when she finally interviewed the actor, she would 'bust his balloon' and she promised to prove him an ordinary man who puts his trousers on one leg at a time like other men. Her editor agreed to hold important space in their paper's weekend edition for the 'tough' interview that was promised.

She spent two hours with Grant in his hotel suite. They had

tea. He liked her hair. The article she wrote was such a one-sided, gushy love letter that her editor refused to print it. Such was the effect of Cary's charm!

Along with the charm, Grant has always been determined to receive fair financial treatment. Early in his career he often demanded and got special contract concessions that far exceeded those won by his counterparts among young leading men. The Grant determination not to be cheated is perhaps best illustrated by a true story told by one of Hollywood's most credible and popular journalists, Jim Bacon. Bacon described the famous incident in his best-seller, *Hollywood Is a Four-Letter Word*. The story has since been related at cocktail parties around the world.

New York's Plaza Hotel is listed in most travel books as one of the world's most glamorous and luxurious. It was a flagship of the international chain of Hilton hotels. It deals with the idiosyncrasies of movie stars, heads of state, and the most demanding of business travellers. Room service at the Plaza Hotel is itself a great tradition. You can order anything from English tea to a seven-course dinner with the finest of French wines. The prices are ridiculously high, but the service is fast and usually quite congenial.

The menu in each Plaza Hotel room lists English muffins in the plural. However, for years, when you ordered English muffins, you only got three halves. Enter Cary Grant, Movie Star, insistent on high English standards for thrift. Grant ordered the English muffins, listed in the plural. He got three halves.

Since the Plaza charges a fortune even for snacks, when Cary was served only three halves of muffins, he immediately asked the Puerto Rican waiter why. The Puerto Rican waiter had no answer. Either he didn't speak English, or, if he did, he certainly didn't have anything to do with important decisions like how many halves of muffins should be sent to Cary Grant. According to Jim Bacon and others who know the story, Grant got on the phone, complained to room service, and insisted on being told why, when muffins were listed in the plural, he only got 'a muffin and a hawf'.

The room service manager referred him to the assistant manager of the hotel. He didn't know. 'We've always served three slices or halves, ever since I've had this job,' the assistant manager told the star. Grant then called the managing director of the hotel, who said he would gladly send up another half muffin at no charge for Mr Grant, but he did not know why it had always been done that way.

When you're Cary Grant, you call the boss. His next call went to Conrad Hilton's home in Beverly Hills. According to Jim Bacon, Grant was told by a butler that the international hotel man was in Istanbul. When you're Cary Grant, you call the boss, even if he's in Turkey. An hour and a half later, Cary Grant reached Hilton in Istanbul. By that time, Grant's tea was cold and the one-and-a-half English muffins soggy. But at least Hilton had the answer.

It became apparent why Hilton was the owner of the hotel and not the manager, the room service director, or even the waiter. It seems that an efficiency expert had been hired to study the eating habits of guests in the Plaza Hotel. Hilton told Grant that 90% of all guests, when they ordered English muffins, only ate three halves, leaving the fourth half on their plates. The efficiency expert had ordered that the muffin-cutters in the kitchen toss the fourth half into a large container and use it with eggs benedict.

This infuriated Cary Grant, who told Hilton that the menu was misleading. Grant insisted it should list English muffins as 'a muffin and a hawf, not muffins in the plural'. Hilton issued an immediate directive that henceforth all four halves should be served when English muffins were ordered. Cary Grant had spent more than $100 in phone calls, but he tells friends, 'It was worth it.'

More than one journalist, determined to find out whether the story is a true one, has checked into the Plaza and ordered room service. Lo and behold, you get four halves – two whole muffins. Thank you, Cary.

Edward G. Robinson, one of the greatest action actors of all times, died without ever being nominated for an Oscar. The immensely talented Orson Welles never received the coveted award as Best Actor in a film. Despite all his movies which helped others win awards, and the special recognition he had from his peers, Cary Grant never received an Academy Award as Best Actor. Nevertheless, ask actors, film-makers, or audiences, and they will generally agree that Cary Grant is the all-time master of sophisticated screen comedy. If you believe what another fine British actor once said, that 'dying is easy — comedy is hard,' then Cary Grant deserves many awards.

How best to describe the unique Cary Grant image? The star once made a courtroom appearance when doing battle with his former wife, Dyan Cannon, over a matter related to child custody. Both sides were ready to present their arguments and leave the decision to the 'infinite and always impartial wisdom' of the presiding judge in the Beverly Hills, California, courtroom.

Dyan Cannon told me that just as the proceedings were about to begin, the judge abruptly excused himself and returned to his chambers. When Dyan asked the clerk of the court about the delay, he told her that the judge's wife had insisted that he call home and tell her 'how Cary Grant looked that day'. Convinced that she was litigating with a legend and not a mortal man, Dyan capitulated. Grant prevailed without saying a word.

His extraordinary charisma has made too many women wonder why their mates and lovers (or both) can't be more charming, better groomed and more like you know who!

Now at 83 years old, Cary Grant still enjoys talking about Cary Grant. In recent interviews, he paraphrases some of the *bons mots* for which he is famous and occasionally adds a surprise or two. Grant openly admits his age to reporters and he doesn't claim any health or fitness secret for others anxious to learn how to survive eight decades.

Whether he is visiting a New York office or at the races, Grant is still a friendly mingler. He says he has been a star so long that public recognition is just a way of life. He told Diane Shah, one of America's more persistent and thorough journalists, that years ago he 'threw money around to impress people. But then I learned you don't impress people like that. So I

1

'ONLY A MOVIE STAR'

WHAT'S YOUR FAVOURITE Cary Grant film?

There are perhaps no more than a handful of stars about whom we ask each other that question. The short list could include Katharine Hepburn, Humphrey Bogart, Clark Gable, Bette Davis – these are some of the larger than life members of that exclusive club of people we call Movie Stars.

Since the 1930s, Cary Grant has been a charter member of that special club, representing as no one else before or since a special personality, unique image. He was Cary Grant and no one else ever played 'Cary Grant' so well, so convincingly, or so endearingly.

Movie critics, colleagues and fans alike describe him in superlatives. Everyone has their favourite Cary Grant film, whether an Alfred Hitchcock thriller like *Suspicion* or a light comedy like *His Girl Friday*. The connection between all his movies, and the reason he is remembered in that elite club of Movie Stars, is that we always know what character Cary Grant will play when we sit down to watch one of his films. Cary Grant always played Cary Grant. As long as his movies are there to entertain us, fans will never forget or stop loving him.

His public personality was not necessarily the role Grant played in his most private life. But, on the screen, he never let his fans down. We always saw the character we loved and knew and expected, no matter what the role was. This was also true in any public appearance off the screen.

This ability to maintain a unique personality is what he had in common with his fellow members in that elite society of Movie Stars. Katharine Hepburn played Katharine Hepburn no matter what the script, the co-stars or the directors. Ditto for Humphrey Bogart, for John Wayne, for Bette Davis. Even if we don't like the movie, we always like them.

There are undoubtedly those who would argue with his devoted biographer, David Thomson, who called Cary Grant simply 'the best and most important actor in the history of the cinema'. Fewer people will argue with critic Andrew Sarris and others on both sides of the Atlantic who have said Cary Grant was 'the most gifted light comedian in the history of the cinema'.

Who is this Cary Grant that Cary Grant played so well? Late in his career, *Time* magazine said, 'He is the only man in movie history who has maintained himself for more than 30 years as a ranking romantic star. He wears only one expression, the bland mask of drawing-room comedy. He plays only one part, the well-pressed elegantly masculine existence that finds itself splashed by love's old sweet ketchup. He creates in a vacuum of values, he is a technician, but he is a technician of genius.'

Watching Cary Grant on the screen makes the viewer feel better. Critic Pauline Kael says, 'Everybody thinks of him affectionately because he embodied what seems a happier time.' His long-time friend and favourite co-star, Grace Kelly, may have put it best, 'Everybody grows old, everybody except Cary Grant.' Katharine Hepburn said, 'He is a personality functioning.' On screen, nothing ever got Cary Grant down in the end. That was true of his personal life as well, despite several events and circumstances that might have made another man give up.

For all the pleasure he gave us in so many films and playing so many roles, this actor won no Academy Awards until his retirement. Critic Richard Corliss explains that oddity this way: 'Because Cary Grant was never called upon to play Hamlet, except indirectly, applause and Oscars have eluded him. "He's only a movie star." And yet the range of his roles — manic managing editor in *His Girl Friday*, desperate adoptive father in *Penny Serenade*, vulnerable charmer in *North by North-*

west – and the breadth he effortlessly brings to these roles suggest an acting ability as large as it is self-effacing.'

The critics aside, Cary Grant was the audience favourite. The reviewers might pass on a movie, calling it 'just another Cary Grant' comedy. But the cinema-going public showed their opinion at the box office. Picture after picture, year in and year out, a Cary Grant film meant money in the bank to the studio that released it. They're still raking it in through television.

It is only due to our ever-increasing ticket prices and multi-million-dollar productions that a number of Grant's box-office records have recently been broken. When many of his most popular films were made, cinema tickets cost just 25 or 50 cents. Today, they cost five or six dollars. If you adjust for inflation, you can find that Grant's old films compare very favourably to today's box-office receipts. To put it in a nutshell, few actors in the history of film have brought people to the cinema the way Cary Grant has.

In the era that he made his films, the most important movie theatre in the United States was Radio City Music Hall in New York. Its status allowed its management first choice on every film made in Hollywood. Producers would hurry up or delay the release of a picture for weeks or even months if it meant it could play Radio City. Best of all, the ultimate in film releases, was to get a picture into Radio City for the still famous Christmas show.

Twenty-eight Cary Grant movies played Radio City, over a third of all he made. Of this 28, 13 were Christmas show films. In one ten-year period, Grant had eight Radio City Christmas films. Cary Grant's 28 Radio City films are an all-time record. The next highest total is Katharine Hepburn with 22, followed by Fred Astaire with 16.

Grant set box-office records of all kinds. One of his films was the first ever to earn $100,000 in a single week. Another Grant movie was the first ever to earn $100,000 in a single week at a single theatre. The week his *Charade* opened at Radio City for Christmas, 1963, it earned over $175,000 from tickets priced at no more than $2.00 apiece. This single theatre, single week record was rarely matched before the 1980s.

The public's affection for Cary Grant was well demonstrated in 1984. A Chicago newspaper had just been purchased by media baron Rupert Murdoch. Fighting for circulation, the paper published a huge, black-bordered photo of Grant that took up almost its entire front page.

Everyone in Chicago assumed it meant that Grant had died. The whole city went into almost instant mourning. One radio station actually announced that Cary Grant was dead. Not until people opened the paper did they read that the photo was to celebrate the actor's eightieth birthday. When asked to comment that night, he told one television station, 'I never felt better in my life.' He was deeply amused by the story. The paper was forced to apologize for weeks for scaring its readers.

Cary Grant made his first movie in 1932 for Paramount Pictures. He was 28 years old. The film was *This Is the Night*. His last movie, *Walk, Don't Run*, came in 1966 when he was still young at 62.

During all those years and on into his retirement, Cary Grant personified a charm, sophistication, wit and grace unequalled by any other actor.

To several generations of film-goers, he was Hollywood's ideal leading man. Whether his role was opposite Mae West in the comedy *She Done Him Wrong*, in the adventure *Gunga Din*, or flirting with Grace Kelly in Hitchcock's *To Catch a Thief*, women loved him and men wanted to be in his shoes. The characters and situations varied widely, but Cary Grant played each role with the same flair and style. Audiences responded so enthusiastically that 'Cary Grant' has come to define 'Hollywood leading man' as much as Kleenex means facial tissue.

In his later years on the screen, Grant was directed four times by Stanley Donen, who also became Grant's partner in their own production company. Donen remembers, 'Cary was always very easy to direct. He brought a great enthusiasm to each of his projects. Remember, he never had to make a picture. Everything he did was something he wanted to do. He could pick and choose who he wanted to work with and on what projects he worked. He never had to do a film just for the money, or the exposure, or to keep busy. He only worked in films that he wanted to do and with people who were his friends and with whom he shared a mutual respect. It's easy to work under those circumstances.

'He was a perfectionist and very meticulous in everything he did. He was very concerned about every facet of the movie. He wanted everything to be done perfectly. This shows up in the work he did. You can look back over his entire career, and, once he was established, you can't find any really bad films he ever made . . . He took direction well, especially once he had learned to trust you. He understood you were the director and he was the actor.

'He was a truly gifted actor . . . He could play all roles well, not just the debonair man, but . . . everything from slapstick to heavy drama. Each of the four films we did together was a different type of role . . . (He knew) what suited him . . . (If he) didn't think it was right for him, he simply said no.'

Although not necessarily true of his entire professional life, many believe it was these factors which helped Grant maintain his career over more than three decades. He took control fairly early in his professional life. Most great stars of Hollywood's golden age, like Jimmy Cagney, Kate Hepburn, Gary Cooper and Spencer Tracy, experienced wide swings in their careers. The highs were very high, but there were lows during which producers called them 'box-office poison'.

That never happened to Cary Grant. Some of his films were less successful than others, some even lost money, and a few times he took on roles for which he was totally unsuited. But generally speaking, his career progressed steadily, free of any wide swings. In this respect, he was almost alone among Hollywood's movie stars.

A number of the so-called 'Golden Era' greats did their best work very early in their careers and later only went through the motions, living on their reputations for years doing 'character' roles. Grant was still making some of his best films in his later years on the screen. Many would argue his greatest performance was in Alfred Hitchcock's *North by Northwest* in 1959, the 66th film of his career.

One of the hardest things to understand about Cary Grant's career is how long it took for him to be honoured by the film industry. Had there been People's Choice awards while he was making movies, he would have undoubtedly been a winner again and again. The Academy of Motion Picture Arts and Sciences, however, waited for his retirement to honour him.

In March, 1965, screenwriter Peter Stone stepped before the microphones and television cameras to receive his Oscar for writing *Father Goose*. His thanks were simple, and directed towards one man. 'Thank you, Cary,' Stone said. 'You keep winning these things for others.'

And that was the truth. Year after year, film after film, others were nominated or won Academy Awards for films dominated by Cary Grant. Some of the more obvious examples include: Best Actor Jimmy Stewart in *The Philadelphia Story*, Best Actress Joan Fontaine in *Suspicion* and Best Director Leo McCarey for *The Awful Truth*; and nominees like Irene Dunne, also in *The Awful Truth*, and Katharine Hepburn in *The Philadelphia Story*. In Cary Grant's entire career, he was only nominated twice, and never won. While these others deserved their Oscars, he too deserved the honour and recognition.

Part of the problem was (and is) Hollywood's long-standing resistance to recognizing comedy. Few comedy actors receive Academy Awards. Yet, most actors maintain that comedy is more difficult to do than straight drama.

Grant himself agreed with this. As he once put it: 'The secret of comedy is doing it naturally under the most unnatural circumstances. And film comedy is the most difficult of all. At least on the stage you know right away whether you are getting laughs or not. But making a movie, you have no way of knowing. So you try to time the thing for space and length and can only hope when it plays in theatres months later that you have timed the thing right. It's difficult and it takes experience. I'll always remember the great actor, A. E. Matthews, who said on his death bed: "Dying's tough, but it's not as tough as comedy."'

Academy Award historian Bill Libby puts it this way: 'There have been few greater sophisticated actors of comedy than

Cary Grant. But his only two nominations came for serious roles, in *Penny Serenade* in 1941, and *None But The Lonely Heart* in 1944. It is difficult to believe that he was not nominated and did not win at least once for *The Awful Truth, Bringing Up Baby, His Girl Friday, The Philadelphia Story, Suspicion, Talk of the Town, To Catch A Thief* or *North by Northwest*. A master of perfect timing, he deserved an Oscar if anyone did. It was due to snobbery that he was denied one.'

In 1970, although no announcement had ever been made, it was clear that Cary Grant had retired from making movies. So the Academy of Motion Pictures Arts and Sciences decided to make up for a lifetime of snubs by voting him a special Oscar. The award, presented at the Oscar ceremonies on April 7 of that year, read: 'Cary Grant – For his unique mastery of the art of screen acting with the respect of his colleagues.' It was only the third such special Oscar ever voted. The first two went to Greta Garbo in 1954 and to producer Arthur Freed in 1953.

For a man who had spent 30 years hurt and disappointed by the lack of recognition from his peers, it was a highlight of a lifetime. He spent the night before the ceremony practising his acceptance speech. The Oscar was given by Frank Sinatra, who said, 'It is awarded for sheer brilliance of acting. Cary has so much skill he makes it all look so easy.' With tears in his eyes, and remembering his early struggles, Grant thanked his colleagues in a trembling voice.

'You know that I may never look at this without remembering the quiet patience of the directors who were so kind to me, who were kind enough to put up with me more than once, some of them even three or four times. There were Howard Hawks, Hitchcock, the late Leo McCarey, George Stevens, George Cukor and Stanley Donen. And the writers. There were Philip Barry, Dore Schary, Bob Sherwood, Ben Hecht, dear Clifford Odets, Sidney Sheldon and more recently Stanley Shapiro and Peter Stone. Well, I trust they and all the other directors, writers and producers and my leading women have forgiven me what I didn't know. You know that I've never been a joiner or a member of any . . . of a particular social set, but I've been privileged to be part of Hollywood's most glorious era.'

In the years to come, he would be often asked what the most memorable occasions in his life were. The answer was always that the first was the birth of his daughter, Jennifer, in 1966. The second was the special Oscar awarded in 1970. The third was receiving the Presidential Medal from ex-actor Ronald Reagan during the 1981 Kennedy Center Honors.

Grant sat at the right of Reagan, in the Presidential box, his medal gleaming around his neck. His wife Barbara and daughter Jennifer were nearby, as his friend Rex Harrison introduced a short tribute made up of clips from his many films.

'Film audiences of the world,' Harrison began, 'have loved the civilized grace and brilliance of Cary Grant. But perhaps all have not realized that he is one of the most accomplished actors in the history of motion pictures, because civilized grace and comic brilliance are two of the most unique and rare qualities within an actor's range. How wonderful that we have gathered to see this modest man acclaimed and honoured for a lifetime of joyous performances. As we look at you seated in that box we can only feel deep regret that you decided to end your acting career so early. Since your retirement . . . there have been descriptions of many newcomers as "young Cary Grants". The fact is there is only one original, the supremely gifted man, whom we honour tonight for a magnificent career on the screen.'

When the short film retrospective was finished, Audrey Hepburn stepped up to the podium to speak poetically on behalf of his many leading ladies.

'If all the world's a stage and all the men and women merely players, then here's a very special player who has also been our friend. For what is friendship if not a willingness to give? To give laughter where there are tears, comfort where there are fears, pleasure, fantasy and fun where there are none. A friend who brings to our lives often stark, brightness and cheer, sweeping away thoughts sorrowful and dark. Giving us strength to face each day. So, thank you Cary, for giving joy across the years to those who need, in times of selfishness and greed, a star to hang dreams on. And before I'm gone, in gratitude and love I end, you have truly been a friend.'

Retirement brought other honours. The Los Angeles County Art Museum held a retrospective of his films that lasted over 60 days. The Metropolitan Museum in New York did the same. The Friars Club honoured him as its Man of the Year at a fund-raising dinner that sold out 1,200 seats at $1,000 per ticket. MGM renamed its studio theatre after him.

He always found these events difficult. A self-effacing man, throughout his life he introduced himself to strangers with, 'Hello, I'm Cary Grant' – as though he didn't realize he had one of the most recognizable faces in the world. He was uncomfortable with all the personal attention, although deeply gratified.

At the Friars' dinner, after a night of praise, he stepped to the microphones with tears running down his cheeks. He excused this lapse of image by explaining, 'I tear up easily. I cry at great talent, art, music, even at great baseball games. To indulge one's emotions is a privilege allowed the elderly like me.'

Much of our admiration for Cary Grant comes from our love for the character he always portrayed on the screen. Throughout his film career and then into retirement, Cary Grant embodied a particular wit, charm and grace that has never been successfully copied or matched. He had a special sophistication that no actor of his generation or following ones has ever equalled.

Fans knew that whatever the plot or whoever the director or co-stars, they could depend on Cary Grant to play his role with flair and style. Some directors, like Alfred Hitchcock, perhaps did a better job with him than others, some scripts may have been more memorable, some co-stars may have been more famous than others, but Cary Grant never left his basic screen personality out of any of his works.

Other leading men of the Movie Star era – great performers like Henry Fonda, Gary Cooper, James Cagney, Jimmy Stewart – had screen personalities that were said to come from their early private lives and backgrounds.

With Cary Grant, it seems that he developed a screen persona first and then grew into it in real life. He himself said many times, 'Everyone wants to be Cary Grant. I want to be Cary Grant.' He also said, 'I play myself to perfection.' In an interview several years ago, he explained, 'When I appear on the screen, I'm playing myself. It's harder to play yourself. I pretend to be a certain kind of man on the screen and I became that man in life. I became me. But to play yourself – your true self – is the hardest thing in the world to do. Watch people at a party. They're playing themselves like everything, but nine times out of ten the image of themselves they adopt is the wrong one. Adopt the true image of yourself, acquire a technique to project it, and the public will give you its allegiance.' In his case, we certainly have.

In the early 1980s, Cary Grant began a series of personal appearances that he called 'An Evening with Cary Grant'. Most of the Evenings were held in conjunction with film festivals and/or for college or university students. The Evenings began with twenty minutes of clips from his films, followed by a brief lecture from him. The heart of the Evening followed with a session called General Questions, about which Grant would invariably quip, 'Ah, yes, General Questions, I knew him well.'

This question-and-answer period often lasted up to two hours. The audience asked anything they liked and Grant's answers were very candid and frank. In the summer of 1985, Grant appeared for one of these Evenings in Kingston, New York. He was asked if he had simply played himself on screen.

'Yes,' he started to say. Then he paused. 'I don't know. I guess that I just patterned myself on a kind of combination of Jack Buchanan – he was the reigning musical comedy star of those days – and Noel Coward. In other words, I pretended to be somebody I wanted to be until finally I became that person. Or, rather, he became me.'

Cary Grant the man. Cary Grant the actor and performer. Cary Grant the Movie Star. Critic Richard Schickel outlined the progression in his book, *Cary Grant: A Celebration*, published in 1981:

'The persona he constructed deliberately referred to nothing in his life or in the life of his times. Mostly, he played not what he had been, but what as a youth, he wished he could be, not as a remembered reality, but a remembered dream. His screen character was a stylization, based on previous stylizations that he had observed around show business, and although he had become a nominal star within a couple of years after his first screen appearance, he did not become one in the fullest meaning of the term until several years later, when the movies themselves evolved a highly stylized concept, the lunatic 1930s comedy which could encompass this creation of his, give it the proper setting as it were . . . Grant offered no hint of personal history on screen and had to wait and help form an imaginative world in which his great creation could breathe easily and live naturally.'

The suave, debonair sophisticate who was Cary Grant had to be a product of imagination. How he grew up, in real life, was completely the opposite of what he later became. Early experience contributed nothing to the Cary Grant we all loved. That's unless you maintain that a sad, hard childhood can spur imagination and ambition and provide the motivation to give the world one of its favourite, larger-than-life Movie Stars.

2

ARCHIE

ARCHIE – ARCHIBALD ALEXANDER LEACH – was born in Bristol, a city on the River Avon in England, on January 18, 1904. Fortune was not smiling on his birth, in fact the home he came into was decidedly not a happy one. There was no hint of his later life as Cary Grant.

His father was Elias Leach, the son of a local potter. People in Bristol who knew him at the turn of the century describe him as tall and handsome with what Archie would later call a 'fancy' moustache. Outwardly Elias seemed cheerful but quiet, although years later his son would say, 'He had a sad acceptance of the life he had chosen.'

A tailor's presser by trade, he worked for many years for the same firm, Todd's Clothing Factory near Portland Square. He earned a basic living, enough to put a roof over his head and decent food on the table. But it was only enough for life's necessities. There was a very little left over for luxury.

Mrs Leach was the former Elsie Kingdon. A local girl, she was the youngest of a large family. She was small and thin, and usually described as shy. Outward appearances were deceiving, though, as later events would prove. She had both a fierce determination and a sharp temper.

While her four brothers went off to Canada to seek their fortunes, Elsie stayed at home to care for her ageing parents. By the time she was 21 years old, she'd decided she wanted to start her own family. She picked Elias Leach, then 25, to help her reach that goal. They were married on May 30, 1898, in the parish church.

At the time, some people thought she was marrying beneath herself. Her father was a successful shipwright. But Elsie thought that Elias had promise. She believed she could help him make something of his life.

They moved into a small rented house at 30 Brighton Street, about a mile north of the centre of Bristol. It was a simple, terraced house – square, brick, gas-lit. Heat came from small coal fires and from the large stove in the kitchen. Elias planted both flowers and vegetables in the back garden.

The Leaches seemed to be a happy and content young couple, but Elsie was ambitious, much more so than poor Elias. He worked as hard as he could, agreeing to as much overtime as they would give him at Todd's, but there never seemed to be enough money. Elsie's worries increased when she found herself pregnant.

The baby, John William Elias, was born on February 9, 1899, one day after Elsie's twenty-second birthday. It was an exceptionally happy time for them, sadly a time that would never again be repeated.

Elsie adored her new son. She doted on him, coddled him, and watched his every move with love. He was sickly from the very beginning, with terrible bouts of severe coughing and fever. Today, the baby would probably be diagnosed as asthmatic. His condition was worsened by the coal fires in the Leach home. It led to tubercular meningitis. Elsie nursed him day and night, but he only got worse. She drove herself to exhaustion.

On February 6, 1900, the doctor examined baby John. He told Elsie she was doing all that she could and demanded that she get a decent night's sleep. She did so. When she woke up the next morning her baby was dead. He was just two days short of his first birthday.

Elsie blamed herself. Had she stayed awake with him, she might have been able to bring him through another night. The child's death changed her. As the days passed, she gave in to fits of melancholy and depression. At the same time, she increased the pressure on her husband. He, in turn, began to drink heavily. It could not be called a happy home.

Elias thought all this might change when, in the late spring of 1903, Elsie told him that she was pregnant again. The Leaches had moved to another house, at 15 Hughenden Road, trying to dim the memory of their tragedy.

If she had prepared for the birth of her first baby with a single-minded determination, that determination now became an obsession with this new pregnancy. It was in her mind that she had done something wrong the first time, that somehow it was her fault that the baby had not been healthy. She did everything she could think of to be sure that the coming child would not suffer the fate of her first son.

On a cold day in January, Elsie went into labour. Early the next morning, January 18, 1904, the baby was born. Everyone, particularly Elsie, was thrilled when the midwife pronounced the dark-haired boy completely healthy. But Elsie was taking no chances. She refused to allow Elias to register the child's birth for fear that once it became 'official', somehow this infant would be doomed like her first.

Later, when it became clear that this baby was indeed the picture of health, she sent Elias down to the registry in Quaker's Friars. On February 29, 1904, the birth of Archibald Alexander Leach, destined to become Bristol's most famous son, was duly recorded.

If Elsie had prepared for Archie's birth singlemindedly, she now devoted herself to him with even more dedication. He became her whole life. As he grew, she wouldn't let him out of her sight. She kept him in long curls and infant gowns until he was almost three.

She couldn't stop being afraid. She was sure that somehow, if Archie were not at her side every moment, fate would intervene and he would suffer the same end as her first son. She announced she would not have any more children. This child was to be her entire life.

Elias had hoped that having a healthy child would allow the family to return to normal. It did not. Elsie all but shut him out of her life as her relationship with Archie obsessed her. Elias was only there to bring home his pay. No matter how hard he worked, how much overtime he collected, it was never enough.

The truth was, Elias did not mind his long hours at the clothing factory. They kept him out of the house and away from his wife's nagging. After work, he usually went to a local pub and didn't return home until late at night. Little Archie hardly ever saw his father.

At one point, Elias took what he thought was a better job. The factory made khaki army uniforms. It was located in Southampton, some 90 miles from Bristol. He took the job for two reasons: more money and, the truth be known, to get away from Elsie.

The people at Todd's were sorry to see him go. His workmates even had a collection to buy him a gold pocket-watch. It became his most treasured possession. Years later, he gave it to his son, who kept it ever since.

Even though he made more money at the Southampton job, the extra income was being eaten up by having to maintain two homes. So Elias returned to Bristol, to Todd's – and to Elsie. Todd's was delighted to have him back. Elsie said she didn't care one way or the other.

As an only child, little Archie had no brother or sister to turn to, no companion to help him escape from the unhappy, angry environment his parents created, nor from the singleminded attentions of his mother.

Elsie remained totally dedicated to Archie. As he grew, she gave him singing and dancing lessons. Even though they had little money, she engaged a piano teacher for him. Every day, Elsie and young Archie would take long walks in the afternoon on the downs, along the River Avon and into the more affluent neighbourhoods of Clifton where she herself had been born. During these walks, she would talk to him about wealth and success. Much of his later ambition and his aversion to poverty was probably born during these walks.

In those days, children started school at five. But Elsie believed her Archie was gifted. So, when he was four-and-a-half, she sent him off to Bishop Road Junior School to start his education.

There was never enough money in the Leach household. Much later in life, Archie/Cary would tell an interviewer, 'My father progressed too slowly to satisfy my mother's dreams. The lack of sufficient money became an excuse for regular sessions of reproach, against which my father learned the futility of trying to defend himself.'

In 1911, when Archie was seven, the family moved again, this time to a new and much larger house at 5 Seymour Avenue. Elias did not want to take on the more expensive home, but Elsie insisted. Two young women, cousins of Elsie's, moved in with them, in part to help pay the higher rent and in part to provide Elsie with some company.

At the time, Archie's schoolwork was at best indifferent, but he did discover sports. He was a terrific soccer goalie. He also discovered films and especially loved the adventure serials that were shown at the local cinema each weekend. By the time he was nine, his studies had improved. With the constant encouragement of his mother (some would say at her insistence) he began applying himself to see if he could win a scholarship to a better school.

Life at home continued to deteriorate. Elsie did not like sharing Archie with his school friends. She became even more protective. She wanted to control his life absolutely – from what he wore to where he went. Elias, on the other hand, approved of Archie's sports and activities and was no doubt delighted that he was getting away from Elsie. This led to continued friction between Elias and Elsie. Archie saw himself as its cause.

The two even disagreed about where their son should see films and with whom. Elias would take the boy and some of his friends to the Metropole, a large barn-like cinema frequented by working people. The audience yelled and screamed at the screen, cheering the hero and booing the villain. When his mother took Archie to a film, she insisted they go alone to the more expensive and exclusive Clare Street Cinema, where patrons sat in wicker armchairs and took tea and cakes as they watched the films with utmost decorum.

As Archie's ninth birthday came and went, the Leach household became even stranger. Elsie had never allowed Archie to wear trousers saying that young gentlemen wore shorts and starched collars. By now, Archie was about the only nine-year-old in Bristol still in shorts. One day a tremendous family fight took place with Elias demanding that his son be given trousers and Elsie resisting.

Finally Elsie gave in, but she insisted on making them herself, although Elias could have bought them from Todd's very cheaply. The trousers she made fitted very badly. Elias accused her of doing it on purpose. She denied it and insisted Archie wear these or none at all. He wore them, immensely relieved to be out of shorts. Any trousers, whether they fitted or not, were fine with him.

Elias began to have bouts of depression. He stayed away from home more and more. In response, Elsie got stranger and stranger. She became more obsessive. She hoarded food. She wandered through the house asking no one in particular where her dancing-shoes were. She sat in front of the fire for hours, just staring. Sometimes she would scrub her hands for minutes on end, again and again. It was clear that her mind was going over the edge.

Elias became concerned. He consulted the family doctor and other officials. Finally one day, without telling Archie, he went into the local magistrates' court and had Elsie committed to Fishponds, the local mental hospital. The next day, he stayed home from work to wait for the hospital people, the men in the white coats.

When Archie came home from school, he found an empty house, his mother strangely absent. He was told simply that Elsie had 'gone away for a rest'.

Mental health care in the early 1900s was primitive. Today, a woman in Elsie's condition would probably be confined for a short period and given medication and counselling. She might be returned home having acquired the means to function, to cope and maybe to find some happiness.

But this was 1913. The breakthroughs in psychiatry that might have helped Elsie Leach return to a productive life were still decades away. Although Elias told Archie that his mother would return shortly, it was obvious before long that she would never come back to the house in Seymour Avenue.

In fact, Elsie never saw her husband again. It was more than 20 years before she saw her son again. Many years after this tragic day, the man who became Cary Grant, the self-assured, successful leading man who was envied by millions, would admit that in his youth, he sometimes blamed his mother for her absence, or his father for allowing the sadness, or himself for not being able to make himself or his parents any happier.

Elsie's leaving marked the start of a particularly unhappy time. As difficult as life had been, it got worse. With Elsie gone, her two cousins soon moved out of the big house in Seymour Avenue. Elias could not afford its upkeep on his own. He and Archie moved in with his mother who lived in Picton Street, a narrow lane of small terraced houses near the centre of Bristol.

Grandmother Leach did not open her arms and welcome the virtually motherless boy into a warm, caring family life. The boy and his father were treated more or less like boarders in a stranger's house. Archie's life was even more unhappy than it had been.

Elias and Archie occupied the front downstairs living-room and a back upstairs bedroom while the elder Mrs Leach kept to herself in a larger upstairs bedroom in the front of the house. They saw very little of each other. Weekend meals were about the only time they were actually together.

During the day, Elias Leach went to work and Archie went to school. Since his father never got home until late in the evening, Archie was left to cook his own dinner and put himself to bed. The nine-year-old boy was basically on his own, a lonely forerunner of today's latch-key child.

Being alone was a very new thing for Archie. Up until now, he'd been the single object of his mother's smothering attention. He took to walking the streets, spending a lot of time on the quay. Hour after hour he would watch the ships heading out into the Channel, wishing he were on one, and dreaming of the day he could leave.

One day he decided to run away from home, a stowaway on one of the departing ships. He started out, but as night came, he lost his nerve and returned home. He kept the dream of signing onto a ship one day as a cabin boy. During this period he got into a little trouble with the authorities. It was not that he was particularly rebellious or delinquent, but he had a lot of time on his hands and was bored. As a result he got into mischief.

School was now Fairfield Secondary, one of the better schools in the area. In those days, a child would go first to an elementary school which would be free for all, and then possibly to a semi-private grammar school which charged fees. The secondary schools filled the gap between the two, sending some of their leavers along to the grammar schools while others went into trade schools or out to find jobs in the factories. Archie had studied hard and had won one of the 'free places' at Fairfield.

Fairfield today stands exactly where it did when Archie Leach went there so long ago. He is well remembered by his contemporaries, and not just because he later became Cary Grant. With no mother at home to look after him, he is remembered as a slightly scruffy boy, rather quiet, as someone who studied carefully but did not achieve high marks. His favourite subjects were geography and history. Grant later admitted that when he entered Fairfield, he hoped that if he worked hard and won scholarships he could go on to grammar school and then to university.

These hopes soon faded. As it was, his father could barely afford the uniform of cap, tie and blazer that boys at Fairfield were required to wear, or the modest fees for books that even free place-holders had to pay. Face to face with economic reality, Archie soon put aside his ambition for education.

Before long, his attention began to turn away from school. Scouting had just begun in England and a troop was started in Bristol in the YMCA Hall in St James's Square. The troop met twice a week, on Wednesday evenings and on Saturdays, for drills called 'exercises'. Once a month, on Sunday morning after church, the 40-odd boys aged ten to 17 assembled dressed in their green sweaters and brown shorts for a parade through the centre of town. In later years, Archie's scoutmaster, Bob Bennett, remembered him as an 'ordinary bloke', usually cheerful, 'although a bit of a loner'. But Archie was enthusiastic and truly enjoyed the exercises and parades.

When the Great War was declared in 1914, many of the troop's older boys immediately left to join the army. The younger boys were given duties at home. Archie became a junior air raid warden.

At the end of his second year at Fairfield, he volunteered for war work. He spent the summer in Southampton working on the docks as a messenger and living with friends of his father's. Although only thirteen, the experience of watching the cream of British youth leaving for France to die in the trenches changed him. When he returned to school in the autumn, he had lost interest in his studies and his old life. He knew his future did not lie in Bristol.

Shortly after starting his third year at Fairfield, Archie discovered the Bristol Hippodrome and its entertainers. A part-time instructor in Fairfield's chemistry lab had taken a liking to Archie, partly because, although his schoolwork was not particularly good, he loved chemistry, especially lab work. The man was actually an electrician by trade. He had designed and installed the Hippodrome's electrical system, replacing its gas lighting.

One Friday, the man invited Archie to come with him to Saturday's matinee and to see what went on backstage. Archie jumped at the chance, not so much because he cared about singing and dancing, but because he was curious about electricity. He watched the first show from the wings.

In later years, he used the word 'destiny' to describe how that afternoon changed his life. It was love at first sight. He instantly knew what he wanted. He later recollected, 'I found myself in a dazzling land of smiling, jostling people. They were wearing all sorts of costumes and doing all sorts of clever things. And that's when I knew. What other life could there be but that of an actor?' It's not difficult to understand how attractive the gaiety and liveliness of the theatre must have seemed to a boy who had never known real joy at home.

At the time, there were three music halls in Bristol. The Hippodrome was the largest and featured spectacular productions like those of the biggest entertainment houses in London. The Empire was about half the size of the Hippodrome and featured a new kind of show just coming into vogue, called a 'review'. The third, the Theatre Royal, was all but out of bounds because it was located in an extremely tough neighbourhood. It was a small, traditional music hall.

After that first afternoon, Archie began to haunt both the Hippodrome and the Empire. Occasionally he would even sneak over to the Theatre Royal to see a particular show. Soon he was giving short shrift both to school and his scout troop. Young Archie Leach was in love with the stage, a love that would last a lifetime.

The stage crews of both theatres liked the boy and soon he was running errands for them. This led to a more official, but still unpaid, job as an assistant to the lighting crew at the Empire.

Even though unpaid, young Archie didn't keep his new job very long. One day he focused a spotlight on the stage during an illusionist's act. This was 'The Great Devant, Illusionist Extraordinaire'. Unfortunately, the misdirected spotlight made it perfectly clear to the audience how the Great Devant did the trick with mirrors. It had been the illusionist's best trick. Archie Leach lost his first job. He was barred from the Empire's backstage.

He went back to the Bristol Hippodrome, where he had made his first friends in the business. He hung around backstage, being a 'go-fer'. He was still unpaid, although we might assume he got a tip from time to time. He ran messages, fetched food and tobacco and generally made himself agreeable.

Before long, the Hippodrome offered him a formal job. It didn't pay much, but it did pay. He was the 'call boy'. His job was to go to actors' dressing-rooms to let them know when they were needed on stage. He loved the job and it became the centre of his whole life.

The only fly in Archie's ointment was that he couldn't work the Wednesday matinee. He had to go to school. The solution was simple. He played hooky on Wednesday afternoons. No one at home really cared. His father was never there and his grandmother just wasn't interested in anything the boy did.

Archie's *real* home was the Hippodrome. Its actors and crew had become his family.

One day a new act arrived at the Hippodrome and Archie met the man who would change his life. Bob Pender was an entertainer whose father used to tour Britain putting on shows on a small portable wooden stage. From there, the young Pender had gone on to the music halls. Now a perpetually cheerful man of 46, for nearly a decade he had been running a popular troupe of boys who did slapstick comedy and acrobatics under the name of Pender's Knockabout Comedians. Archie thought these were the luckiest boys in the whole of Britian. He desperately wanted to join them.

During Pender's run at the Hippodrome, Archie overheard him talking to the manager about a problem. World War One, the 'war to end all wars', was claiming the young men in the company to fight once they came of age. There was a constant need for fresh youngsters as others went off to help the war effort. Archie thought this could be his big chance.

When Pender and his troupe moved on to their next engagement, Archie secretly wrote to him in his father's name. He enclosed a photograph of himself, showing him to be a well-built young man who looked older than his actual thirteen years. He asked to join the troupe.

Pender liked the boy's looks. He wrote back to Elias agreeing to take on his son as an apprentice and enclosing the train fare so he could join the troupe in Norwich. Elias never saw the letter. Archie intercepted it before his father got home from work.

The next morning, Archie watched his father leave, then packed his things and hurried to the station. He bought a ticket for Norwich and a few hours later presented himself to Pender at the Theatre Royal there. Pender immediately recognized him as the boy from backstage at the Bristol Hippodrome. Years later, he recalled that he also realised that Archie was younger than he said he was; and that he had probably written the letter himself.

Pender was used to seeing stage-struck boys. He knew they saw the troupe as a way of escaping an unhappy life. If it was all right with the boy's father, he could stay on as an apprentice.

Archie assured him that it was perfectly all right. So Pender gave him a short contract guaranteeing him room, board and ten shillings a week.

Archie was ecstatic. He was actually going to be paid to go on the stage! The next morning, training began. He was taught acrobatics, tumbling, how to do a prat fall, and how to perform the sketches that were the heart of the act. He learned how to put on make-up and how to face an audience.

The week was quickly over. The troupe moved on to its next stop, Ipswich. Pender told Archie he was learning fast and would be integrated into the act before the two weeks in Ipswich were over. Archie was overjoyed. He was about to make his showbiz debut.

Unbeknownst to Archie, Pender had written a second letter to Elias. He assured him his son had arrived safely and had been accepted into the troupe. He gave him the troupe's schedule for the coming months. The second day in Ipswich, a very angry Elias arrived at the stage door to fetch his young son home. But before Elias could confront Archie, Pender intervened and suggested the two men have a cup of tea and a chat.

In all truth, Elias was not particularly upset with Pender. The man had a good reputation. His letter showed that he cared for his boys and was not trying to put anything over on their families. As the two men talked, it became clear they were both members of the fraternal order of Free and Accepted Masons, at the time the world's largest secret society. There could be few disagreements between two Masons and the men hit it off at once.

The problem was that Archie was simply too young. He had said that he was sixteen. Pender thought this was a fib; he thought the boy was fifteen. He was more than a little surprised to learn Archie was just thirteen.

So the two men came to a quick agreement. Archie would go home to Bristol with his father. When he could legally leave school, at fifteen, he could rejoin the troupe if he still wanted to. Archie was disappointed to leave, but relieved to learn he could come back later. He and his father were on the next train back to Bristol.

Cary Grant later reminisced about this period of his life and admitted he had shortened his wait to rejoin Pender – by getting himself expelled from school.

When he first returned to school, he was a hero. He showed his classmates what he'd learned and bragged of his conquest of the music hall. He took to skipping classes and went back to his semi-official backstage job at the Hippodrome. When he did go to school, he was as disruptive as possible. He was constantly in trouble and got regular canings from Augustus 'Gussie' Smith, the stern headmaster.

Things came to a head in March, 1918, when he was fourteen. Archie and another boy hid in the girls' cloakroom, planning to play a prank. They were discovered, however, by one of the teachers and marched down to Mr Smith's office. This was the last straw.

The next morning the school gathered for prayers and assembly. Decades later, Grant vividly remembered the scene: 'My name was called and I was marched up the steps onto the dais and taken to stand next to Gussie Smith where with a quivering lip that I did my best to control I heard words such as inattentive, irresponsible, incorrigible and a discredit to the school. I suddenly realized I was being expelled in front of the assembled school.' (Fittingly for human nature, after Archie Leach became Cary Grant and Cary Grant became Fairfield's most illustrious former pupil, the school cheerfully and conveniently forgot many of the details about how and why Archie departed its hallowed halls.)

Archie told his father about his expulsion that night when Elias came home from work. It came as no great surprise to him. He knew that Archie had been thinking about when he could rejoin Bob Pender. In a way, Elias was relieved. He was sure Pender would watch closely over Archie. It meant he wouldn't have to. It would also be one less mouth to feed. He would not stand in Archie's way. Less than a week later, with his father's blessing, Archie was again off to join the Pender Troupe. He was just two months past his fourteenth birthday.

Within a week, he felt completely at home. Bob Pender and his wife, Margaret, a former dancer for the Folies Bergère, became the supportive father and mother he had lacked for so many years. Within a month, he was working in the act.

Three months later, the Troupe returned to the Bristol Hippodrome for the first time since Archie had joined them. He was now a fully-fledged member of the Troupe. It was a special thrill to perform for his father and many of his friends from Fairfield. Even Gussie Smith came to see him.

During the week in Bristol, Archie stayed with Elias in the house in Picton Street rather than with the other boys at a hotel. His father was very proud of him and Archie felt closer to him than he had for a long time.

Archie toured Britain with Pender for two years. He learned acting, mime, dancing, acrobatics and even how to walk on stilts. Life with the Troupe was similar to life in a boarding-school. When the Troupe played in London, they stayed at the Pender house in Brixton, South London, sleeping in a dormitory built onto the house. On the road, they stayed in boarding-houses or inexpensive hotels with four boys to a room. They were allowed to eat after the last performance but were expected to be in bed with the lights out by 10pm. In the morning, they were expected to be washed, dressed and at breakfast by 7.30am.

Anyone breaking the rules was fired on the spot. The day was filled with rehearsals and practice and the evenings with performances, except on travel days. The Troupe was very popular. It worked constantly with few days off except for travel. Pender taught Archie a discipline that was to remain with him for the rest of his life.

The routine varied little — work, eat, sleep — broken only by days on the train. Occasionally, when demand for them was high, the Troupe would split into two groups of eight so that it could, in effect, be in two places at once. When this happened, Archie was usually sent with the younger boys to play a secondary house while the older boys played the more prestigious venue.

By 1920, Archie was a veteran. He was sixteen years old. His weekly spending money had been upped to a pound. He now went with the older boys whenever the Troupe was split. At this time, Pender received an invitation to bring eight boys to the US. The engagement was at New York's Globe Theater for producer Charles Dillingham. The show starred a musical comedy star of the day, Fred Stone.

Everyone was excited, everyone wanted to go, but it was only possible for only half the Troupe to do so. Finally, Pender chose the privileged group. Archie Leach was the eighth name on the list. It would be a trip that would change his life.

It's doubtful that anyone on the ship that brought the young lad into New York harbour knew the effect he would have on generations of American movie-goers, or, for that matter, that he would earn a world-wide reputation as the ultimate in sophistication and urbanity. It's unlikely that even young Archie Leach had an inkling of what his future in this sprawling country would be.

British citizens rarely understand the attraction they hold for their former colonists. Americans almost always attribute a sort of poise and confidence to people with an English accent, envying what they see as their 'old-worldliness', while staunchly defending their own 'bigger and better' frontier society. Perhaps some of the personality that Cary Grant was to assume was not so much his invention as it was an acceptance of who and what Americans wanted him to be.

In any event, the tumbling young acrobat Archie Leach was still a long way from becoming the suave, debonair Cary Grant when he sailed past the Statue of Liberty in 1920.

3

BROADWAY BECKONS

Wʜᴇɴ Aʀᴄʜɪᴇ ʙᴏᴀʀᴅᴇᴅ ᴛʜᴇ ocean liner for America, the only way to describe him was excited. He and the Penders embarked in July, 1920, on the fabulous *Titanic's* sister ship, the RMS *Olympic*.

Not too many years previously, he had passed his time staring at ships in port, dreaming of leaving on one of them as a cabin boy. Here he was, sixteen years old, a paid passenger, on his way to America to perform on stage. He was thrilled.

The *Olympic* became an even more exciting place when he saw two newly-weds come aboard for the voyage. They were the world's sweethearts, Douglas Fairbanks and Mary Pickford. Although he was travelling second class, Archie tried to follow Fairbanks everywhere. Fairbanks was gracious and spent time chatting with the star-struck teenager.

Decades later, Grant recalled meeting the legendary actor. 'My great hero was Doublas Fairbanks,' he said. 'I met him on the boat when I first came to America. We played shuffleboard together. I was so impressed. He looked so tan and great I decided always to try to keep a tan going. I found myself being photographed with Mr Fairbanks during a game of shuffleboard and as I stood beside him I tried to tell him of my adulation.' This habit of maintaining a tan stayed with Archie Leach long after he became Cary Grant, a famous movie star himself.

Soon after the Penders and their Troupe arrived in New York, they got some initially disappointing news. Dillingham had changed his mind. Rather than book the Troupe at the Globe, one of New York's premier theatres, he wanted them instead to play the Hippodrome, a monstrous theatre on Sixth Avenue and 43rd Street.

Known to one and all as the 'Hippo', it seated more than 4,500. Its immense stage was the length of almost an entire city block. It had 48 huge dressing-rooms, each named after one of the United States. The Hippo had a resident ballet company of 100, a chorus of 150, plus a backstage crew that numbered more than 800. It rightly called itself 'the largest theatre in the world'.*

Dillingham was staging a new spectacular called *Good Times*, featuring a cast of over a thousand. He felt that Pender's type of physical act was better suited to a house the size of the Hippodrome, where dialogue tended to get lost in the distance. They were expected to do two shows a day, six days a week, with a matinee on Sunday. Among many others, they shared the bill with a herd of elephants and a group of female swimmers who performed in a million-gallon tank.

The Penders were disappointed to be playing the Hippodrome, but there was some encouraging news. *Good Times* was likely to have a longer run than the Globe show they had originally been scheduled to do.

Sure enough, the extravaganza ran for 456 performances. By the time it closed, Archie had explored New York from top to bottom. Among his favourite things were the double-decker buses of the day. He rode on the open upper deck up and down Fifth Avenue for hours on end.

As they had in England, the Penders kept very tight control over the boys. Because of the length of the run, they found a large apartment to stay in rather than a hotel. Each boy had chores to do every day. Archie was often assigned to be the cook. His scout training stood him in good stead here. The Troupe especially liked his stew.

When *Good Times* finally closed in the spring of 1921, the

---

* Visitors to New York today will find this spot now occupied by a vast parking garage called the Hippodrome.

Penders faced a hard decision. They had planned to return to England where they were still very much in demand. But the Troupe had received good notices at the Hippodrome, and this brought offers to play several of the vaudeville circuits then in their heyday. The final decision was influenced by economics. The money they were being offered to remain in the States was much greater than they could have hoped to make in England. They accepted a one-year contract to play the B. F. Keith Circuit. This took them to vaudeville houses up and down the East Coast and as far west as Chicago with stops in between.

The Pender Troupe shared bills with some of the biggest names of the day: Eddie Cantor, Jack Benny, the Marx Brothers, the Foy Family. The tour lasted a year, ending with an extended run at the Palace. This theatre stood on the corner of 47th Street and Broadway in New York. It was the pinnacle of the vaudeville world.

By now, it was the summer of 1922. Pender again had to decide whether to sign up for another run in America or return to Britain. He and Margaret and some of the boys were getting a little homesick. They had been in the US for two years. Pender thought it was time to go home, but not all the boys agreed. Several of them, including Archie, felt their futures were in the United States and they wanted to stay. Although it meant breaking up the Troupe, Pender agreed.

During the two years in America, Pender had been saving the boys' money for them. He now gave them each their share plus the equivalent of their fare home. He and Margaret and a few of the boys set sail for England to put together a new Pender Troupe. Within two years, however, Pender retired from show business to start a small toyshop which he ran until he died in 1939.

Archie was nineteen years old. He was on his own in New York. He had hung around show business for the last ten years, being an entertainer in his own right for the last five. New York did not welcome him with open arms.

To this day, if you dine in a New York restaurant, the chances are very good that your waiter or waitress will be an aspiring actor or singer or dancer. The competition among performers is high. The best and the brightest congregate in this city to get parts and bookings that are seen by the top producers and directors and the most sophisticated audiences.

Archie Leach was no more an instant success than most. He had to struggle just to feed, clothe and shelter himself. In those days the vaudeville houses closed down for the summer. Archie didn't know how he was going to make money that first summer of 1922. One of his friends, John Kelly, supported himself making hand-painted ties. He asked Archie to help him, so his first job that summer was selling Kelly's ties on Fifth Avenue. (John Kelly later went on to win an Academy Award as the costume designer for *An American in Paris*.)

Blessed with good looks, and with a growing circle of friends met in various theatres, Archie found himself in demand as one of the 'extra young men' so necessary to the fashionable dinner parties of that era.

One night, he escorted the star Lucrezia Bori to a Park Avenue dinner party. At table, he was seated next to George Tilyou whose family owned the amusement park on Coney Island. They began to talk about Archie's work with the Pender Troupe. When Tilyou heard that Archie could stilt-walk, he instantly offered him a job carrying an advertising board on stilts on the boardwalk at Coney Island. Archie accepted.

He was paid $3 a day, later raised to $5 when he complained that children were always trying to trip him. He got another rise, to $10 a day at weekends, because of the crowds.

Cary Grant on stilts being a walking placard on Coney Island, that least sophisticated of all New York spots, is a remarkable image. For a young man trying to make a name for himself, it must have been a disappointing time. He persevered, however. With the $45 a week he made stilt-walking, and a little extra he got for selling tickets at the Tunnel of Love from time to time, coupled with the continuous flow of dinner invitations, Archie made it through the first summer in New York in fairly good style.

When September came and the vaudeville houses reopened, Archie was anxious to get back on stage. With Tommy Pender, Bob's younger brother, he formed a stilt-walking act called 'The Walking Stanleys'. Another extravaganza was being mounted at the Hippodrome, called *Better Times*, and the boys found themselves back at work.

Better Times ran for almost six months. During that time, Archie and Tommy often met other ex-members of the Pender Troupe who had stayed in New York. They talked about putting together their own act, modelled on what they did with Pender. When *Better Times* closed early in 1923, they had rehearsed and were ready to go on stage with the act.

They tried to get a contract with the Keith Circuit, but couldn't. Instead, they were booked for the Pantages Circuit, a secondary string of vaudeville houses and music halls spread across Canada and down the West Coast of the United States.

On the road again, the new troupe worked its way across Canada, playing four and sometimes even five shows a day, until they got to Vancouver. From there, they started down the West Coast of the US, Seattle, Portland, San Francisco, until they ended up in Los Angeles.

After a four-week run at the Pantages Theatre in LA, the boys could reverse their steps and play their way north up the coast and east across Canada again. But by now, they were all tired of the grind. Archie especially had come to realize that they were really getting nowhere fast. So the Troupe split up and Archie took a train back to New York. He faced another summer there looking for work.

Archie acknowledged a simple truth. He had been on the stage for almost five years, yet he had never spoken a single line to an audience. He also knew that performers who spoke lines earned a lot more money than acrobats or stilt-walkers. Back in New York, he was bound and determined to get a speaking role.

It wasn't easy. The only work he found was doing bit parts in vaudeville acts. In one, he was an audience 'plant' in a mind-reading act. In another, he was a narrator who rose centre stage out of a trap door, dressed in tights, to tell the audience what they were going to see that evening.

One night, the stage elevator got stuck and he couldn't go up or down. In the best tradition of 'the show must go on', Archie spent the rest of the show with his head sticking up on stage as the chorus line danced around him – very carefully.

Actually, he wasn't doing all that badly. He lived in a small room at the Vaudeville Artists Club on 46th Street and worked pretty steadily. In between jobs, he went back to Coney Island, sometimes as a lifeguard and other times as a boardwalk 'barker', standing outside shows and enticing passers-by to come in.

Then Archie got a job as a comedian's straight man and toured around the country. Years later he wrote, 'Eventually I played practically every small town in America. I learned to time laughs. When to talk into an audience's laughter. When to wait for the laughs. When not to wait for the laughs. In all sorts of theatres, playing to all types of people.'

It was a living, but more important, it was training, training that years later would serve him well on the sound stages of Hollywood. Almost two years had passed since he had left Pender. He was 23 years old and that big break in his career had still not come his way.

In New York, when not at one of the dinner parties for which he was still very much in demand, he usually ate at Rudley's Cafeteria, a show business hangout at the corner of 41st and Broadway. Almost every evening a group of young actors, writers and aspiring directors met at Rudley's to eat and to gossip about the business.

It was good company. Besides Archie Leach who went on to become Cary Grant, the group included:

Moss Hart, who became a playwright and screenwriter known for such hits as *The Man Who Came to Dinner*, and who won a Tony Award for directing *My Fair Lady* on Broadway.

George Murphy, who danced his way through Broadway and onto the screen, and in 1964 was elected to the US Senate from California, defeating Pierre Salinger.

Humphrey Bogart, one of Hollywood's most famous movie stars of all time.

Archie's friends spent a lot of time trying to convince him of something he already knew in his heart to be true: vaudeville was dying.

It seemed to him his only future lay in playing revues like the 'Follies' which were quickly starting to replace vaudeville. But he also recognized that he really didn't have the singing voice or the dancing talent that were needed. His friends convinced him that his only future lay on the legitimate stage.

Then one night at Rudley's, Max Hoffman, an up-and-coming musical comedy star, introduced him to Reggie Hammerstein. Reggie was a young stage director; their meeting was a stroke of luck that would change Archie's life. Despite Archie's doubts, Reggie Hammerstein believed that he could have a future in musical theatre. Reggie persuaded him to get some professional training. For the next few months, Archie Leach studied voice, singing and acting.

During that time, he no longer had to wear stilts around Coney Island to support himself. He had a stage job. Jean Dalrymple was an actress and singer appearing in vaudeville with a sketch called, 'The Woman Pays'. Archie had a part in the sketch for which he was paid $75 a week.

After several months, Hammerstein thought Archie was ready for bigger things. Reggie's uncle was Arthur Hammerstein, a noted stage producer who launched, among others, his famous nephew, Reggie's brother, Oscar Hammerstein II.

Arthur Hammerstein was about to open a new Broadway theatre named after himself. His first production there was to be *Golden Dawn*, an operetta written by nephew Oscar. Reggie went to work on Uncle Arthur and persuaded him to sign Archie for the show. He got a small part as an Australian prisoner of war and was the understudy for the juvenile lead. In a way, the role was perfect for Archie. When they first met him, many people thought he was Australian because of his rather strange accent. In fact, one of his nicknames was 'kangaroo'.

According to his contract, he was paid $350 a week, his largest salary to date. This was no small sum in 1927 when a new Model-T Ford was just $895 and the average annual income in the USA was $2,800.

Archie Leach had put his feet on the road to success, and much of the credit had to go to Reggie Hammerstein. In later years, Cary Grant would say of his help, 'It was the nicest thing anyone ever did for me.'

After a month of on-the-road try-outs, *Golden Dawn* opened the Hammerstein Theatre on November 30, 1927, to very mixed reviews. While they panned the show itself, most critics praised the cast, including Archie whom they called 'a promising newcomer'. To the Hammersteins' pleasant surprise, the public, as is so often the case, ignored the critics. The show ran for more than six months and 184 performances. Each night, it seemed Archie developed more confidence. Several times during the run, he stepped in as an understudy and did well.

Arthur Hammerstein was pleased with the work Archie did in *Golden Dawn* and immediately signed him to a long-term contract. He was in Hammerstein's next production, another musical, *Polly*. The star of the show was Fred Allen, who later went on to become a national institution as a comedian on American radio. *Polly* was a restaging of a musical that had been put on in London a decade before. Archie played the role which had been taken by Noel Coward in London.

From the very beginning, *Polly* was troubled. Not even the talents of Fred Allen, then one of the biggest names from vaudeville, could rise above what was obviously not a good show. It got scathing reviews on its first try-out in Baltimore and despite a hurried rewrite, got even worse notices at its next stop, Wilmington, Delaware. When Archie himself got poor reviews in Wilmington, he was replaced before the show reached Broadway. Once there, it lasted only 15 performances.

Archie's disappointment at being replaced was softened somewhat by the fact that he had a six-week guaranteed contract. While *Polly* languished in Wilmington, Archie returned to New York, comfortable with the fact that his $250-a-week cheque would continue for another month.

Then he got a lucky break, one that made being fired from *Polly* seem like a blessing in disguise.

The famous Marilyn Miller was just starting rehearsals as the star of Florenz Ziegfeld's new musical, *Rosalie*. Marilyn Miller had been on stage since she was five. Her first real fame came from starring in Ziegfeld's Follies. Throughout the 1920s, she was one of Broadway's brightest stars. Because of her tragic death by poisoning at the age of 37 (just a few years after being impressed with Archie Leach), she was portrayed in film biographies by both June Haver and Judy Garland.

Miller was unhappy with her leading man for *Rosalie* and thought she knew who would be perfect for the role — that young actor in *Golden Dawn*, Archie Leach. She persuaded the Ziegfelds to ask the Hammersteins to release Archie from his contract so he could join her.

When this luminary wanted Archie Leach to be her new leading man, he was desperately anxious to comply. He saw it as his big break.

In those days of the great, powerful theatrical dynasties, the Ziegfelds and the Hammersteins were the top of the heap and were sworn enemies. The very thought of doing something helpful for the Ziegfelds sent shivers of horror through the Hammersteins' collective spines. They would never release him to their rivals. Arthur Hammerstein and Flo Ziegfeld personally loathed each other.

The Hammersteins were no longer thrilled with Archie Leach. They saw his wanting to work with Marilyn Miller as a defection and proof positive of disloyalty. So when J. J. and Lee Shubert came along and asked for him, they readily sold Archie's contract.

The Shuberts, a theatrical dynasty themselves, had also seen Archie in *Golden Dawn* and had become interested in him. At first, Archie was depressed at being denied his big break, but things worked out well. His relationship with the Shuberts was a happy one, with progressively bigger parts and more money.

The Shuberts offered him a two-year contract at $350 a week, but he surprised them by refusing the long-term agreement. He wanted to be available to do a non-Shubert project if it came up. He was learning from experience. He asked for a run-of-the-show contract. The Shuberts were impressed that he had enough faith in himself to pass up a long-term deal with a guarantee.

His first role with the Shuberts was in a play called *Boom*

Boom, opposite Jeanette MacDonald. MacDonald's film career was soon to take off, starring in a famous series of movies opposite Nelson Eddy.

With his dark good looks, Archie found himself cast as a Spaniard and forced in the big scene to do a fandango with MacDonald. The musical was quite simply awful. It lasted just 72 performances. One critic said of it: 'It can teach one more about despair than can the most expert philosopher.' Of Archie's performance, MacDonald would say many years later, 'He was absolutely terrible in the role but everyone loved him. He has so much charm.'

Even this cloud had a silver lining for Archie. Several weeks before *Boom Boom* opened, Metro-Goldwyn-Mayer (MGM) studios released the first of the all-talking musical movies, *Broadway Melody*, and it was an instant sensation. Now all the studios were suddenly desperate to find musical actors and actresses to bring to Hollywood. Just after *Boom Boom* opened, Paramount asked Archie and Jeanette to come to Astoria Studios in Queens, New York, for a screen test.

Archie was of two minds about the screen test. He still loved films and had liked California and Hollywood during his brief stay there playing the Pantages. On the other hand, he felt that with his new contract with the Shuberts, his Broadway career was starting to take off. He hoped to do well, but was afraid of what decision he might have to make if he did.

In the end, there was nothing to worry about. Paramount loved MacDonald and immediately offered her a contract. But to Archie they said, 'You're bow-legged and your neck is too thick.'

This story is reminiscent of the famous verdict on Fred Astaire's screen test: 'Can't act. Slightly bald. Can dance a little.' It makes one wonder what eventually happened to the short-sighted people who made these early judgments.

So, it was back to the Shuberts. Archie's next show, *A Wonderful Night*, did somewhat better, playing 125 performances. *A Wonderful Night* was a rewrite of Strauss' *Die Fledermaus*. Archie played an overdressed, superficial young man. The play's reviews made those for *Boom Boom* look good by comparison, but the public didn't seem to mind. Perhaps people wanted to take their minds off the stock market crash which happened the day before the show opened.

Straight after *A Wonderful Night*, the Shuberts put him in the road company of *The Street Singer*, opposite Queenie Smith. The tour lasted over nine months, until the spring of 1931. Archie's baritone voice was never more than mediocre but he more than made up for his deficiencies as a singer with his personality, charm, wit and the stage timing he had learned in those long years in vaudeville. The critics may have been indifferent but audiences clearly adored him.

When the *Street Singer* tour ended, the Shuberts immediately sent him to St Louis to play summer stock in the Municipal Opera there. He played 87 nights in different repertory productions in the outdoor theatre.

During that summer, he became friendly with the Midwestern correspondent for the show business newspaper, *Variety*, who wrote a long and glowing piece about the darkly handsome young actor. The *Variety* article turned out to be another lucky break for Archie.

It must be remembered that this was the middle of the Great Depression. Millions of people were out of work, but Archie Leach stayed continuously employed. He made anything from $300 to $450 a week at a time when men would have been delighted to get a job for $100 a week to support their families. On his salary, Archie was able to live very well and even save money. He allowed himself the luxury of a Packard Phaeton convertible touring car, which became his pride and joy.

Given the poverty of his youth, and the hard times all around him, Archie was extremely money-conscious. He was determined, above all else, that he would never be poor again. So when the Shuberts came to the cast in St Louis and asked that they all take a pay cut, Archie not only refused, but at the end of the summer when he returned to New York, he demanded a rise for his next Shubert production.

It was a case of history repeating itself. Archie Leach was again charged with disloyalty. The Shuberts disliked this money demand. They didn't think he was a team player. The

Hammersteins had thought he was disloyal for asking to work for Flo Ziegfeld; similarly, now the Shuberts no longer felt committed to keeping Archie around.

Along came William Friedlander, another Broadway producer. He had seen the complimentary article about Archie in *Variety* and has sent a scout to look at him in St Louis. Friedlander was getting set up to mount a major production of a new musical, *Nikki*, written by John Monk Saunders for his actress wife, Fay Wray. Getting good reports from his scout in St Louis, Friedlander approached the Shuberts about lending him Archie for *Nikki*. They refused at first, but then angered by his demand for a rise, they agreed.

In *Nikki*, Archie played opposite Fay Wray as Cary Lockwood, an American aviator in Paris at the end of World War I. The story was loosely based on a popular magazine series and had already been made into a motion picture by First National with Richard Barthelmess playing the role of Lockwood. The play opened at the Longacre Theatre on September 29, 1931, to generally favourable reviews, but fell victim to the times. People just didn't have the money to go to the theatre. Despite heroic efforts to keep it going, it closed after just 39 performances.

During the month-long run of *Nikki*, another break came Archie's way. A young film director at the Astoria Studios, Casey Robinson, had seen Archie's screen test with Jeanette MacDonald. He thought he had promise, bow legs and thick neck notwithstanding.

Robinson was about to start a quick, one-reel short for Paramount called *Singapore Sue*. He needed four actors to play sailors on leave opposite Chinese actress, Anna Chang. Remembered mainly as a screenwriter, Robinson's future film credits were to include *Captain Blood*, *Dark Victory*, *Now, Voyager*, and *The Corn is Green* with Bette Davis.

When he called Archie to play one of the sailors, Archie quickly agreed. It was only a few days of work, but it meant some extra money, and by this time he was beginning to feel that his future might lie in films. Following that Astoria screen test, Jeanette MacDonald had been given the female lead in

Paramount's *The Love Parade*. The film went on to receive an Academy Award nomination for Best Picture of 1930 and instantly established her as a rising Hollywood star. Archie felt that the one-reeler would give him some exposure to film-making.

Singapore Sue was shot at Astoria in less than a week. It was rapidly edited and sent to California. Robinson liked what he saw in Archie, and liked his work. He wrote a letter to Paramount executives praising Archie and suggesting that they look at his work in the film.

Nothing came of it. When the finished film reached California, it was all but forgotten. In fact the film itself was not released until late in 1932 after a new talent, Cary Grant, had already appeared in several films. *Singapore Sue* was to be the only film credit ever earned by Archie Leach.

For some time Archie had been planning a golfing vacation with his friend, Phil Charig. Charig was a young writer and composer who had some Hollywood connections. The two had planned to go to Florida as soon as both had time available. With the closing of *Nikki* on October 31, 1931, Archie had the time and so did Phil. They began packing. Then his *Nikki* co-star, Fay Wray, called. She had just signed a contract to go to Hollywood to make a movie about a big ape. (Not long afterwards, in 1933, the movie *King Kong* was released, in which Wray played her most famous role as the frightened, struggling, sweet young thing, the object of an infatuated gargantuan gorilla who carried her to the top of the Empire State Building.)

Wray suggested that Archie visit California. He and Phil conferred and agreed that there were as many golf courses in California as in Florida. They decided to go. Given the dismal result of his first screen test, plus the fact that nothing had come from his appearance in *Singapore Sue*, Archie did not really hope for much from Hollywood.

He planned to take a look at the movie scene, to enjoy himself, to play a little golf, and then to return to New York to resume his stage career. The Shuberts had got over their pique about his salary demands and had told him they wanted him to start rehearsals on another project sometime after the New Year.

In the middle of November, 1931, with no great expectations, Archie and Phil Charig loaded up the Packard convertible and set off for California. The man admitted in later years that he was kidding himself. He had the movie bug. The 'vacation' was really a scouting trip. He wanted to be a Movie Star.

4

'IF THIS ONE CAN TALK, I'LL TAKE HIM'

ARCHIE LEACH'S ENTRÉE TO Hollywood turned out to be as
smooth as silk.

While his struggle to become an entertainer had been tough,
from his early days in Bristol to the stilt-walking on Coney
Island through a shaky start on the legitimate stage, his acceptance in Hollywood came easily. Apparently the Fates decided
he had already 'paid his dues', and they smiled on his hopes in
California.

After a leisurely ten-day drive, mostly with the convertible
top down so they could get a tan, Archie and Phil Charig
arrived in California shortly before the Thanksgiving holiday
in November, 1931. They checked into a suite in the fabled
Chateau Elysée, the hotel where so many Broadway actors
first went when they reached California.

Archie was determined to enjoy this vacation in style. He
had worked hard with no time off for almost three years, he
had saved his money, and he was now ready to spend a little.

Between them, the two men knew quite a few people in
Hollywood. Charig had already been there several times on
writing assignments. Archie knew a number of Broadway
actors and actresses who had migrated West.

Almost before they could unpack, the two were plunged
into a fast social whirl. They went to dinner parties almost
every night. When they weren't playing golf, one of their
regular stops was San Simeon.

William Randolph Hearst, the publishing mogul, had fallen

in love with a struggling young actress in 1917. Her name was Marion Davies. Unable to get a divorce from his wife, Hearst nonetheless lived with Davies whenever possible. Together they maintained several homes. Among the most famous was San Simeon, their castle by the sea. Lush, ornate and opulent, it became the setting for frequent Hearst and Davies house parties.

Archie Leach, through Phil Charig, became a regular on San Simeon's tennis courts. There he met Robert Lord, who would later give him important motion picture roles. Lord, a writer and producer, was associated with a great many films throughout his career, notably *One Way Passage* for which he won the Academy Award for original screenplay in 1932.

After about two weeks in California, Archie decided it was time to take a serious look at the movie industry.

Just before he left New York, Billy Grady, a William Morris talent agent, had advised Archie not to sign a new contract with the Shuberts, but rather to see if he could make it in Hollywood. He followed up this advice by setting up an important meeting for Archie in California. The meeting was with Walter Herzbrun, a well-known Hollywood agent. Archie called to arrange an appointment.

Herzbrun was immediately impressed with the young man, who fitted the classic description of tall, dark and handsome. He told Archie, quite frankly, that many had started in Hollywood with a lot less, and said he would introduce him to some people.

Later, he called to say he was lunching the next day with Marion Gering. Herzbrun thought Gering might be able to give Archie some advice about how to break into films. He invited Archie to join them.

Gering had come to the US from Russia in 1924 at the age of 23 as a Siberian fur representative. He soon became a successful director in Chicago and New York. He had recently come to Hollywood to direct movies for Paramount. Gering and Archie hit it off straight away and he turned out to be responsible for Archie Leach's big break in Tinseltown.

Soon after their first meeting, Gering asked Archie to join

him and his wife for dinner with B. P. Schulberg. Benjamin Percival Schulberg had been in the movie business since 1911. He had discovered Clara Bow and made her the famous 'It' girl. He had also discovered Gary Cooper. He was now Paramount's production chief and normally totally inaccessible to aspiring young movie actors. Possessed of a sound memory, he recalled Casey Robinson's recommendation of Archie Leach and looked forward to meeting him.

Cary Grant later recounted what happened at that dinner. Gering talked about his plans to direct a screen test for his wife the next day. Schulberg off-handedly asked Gering to put Archie in that screen test. He told Archie, 'She'll need someone to read against and you can feed her lines. Nothing too difficult.' Gering was game, and so was Archie.

The next day, Archie went to Marathon Street to a Paramount Publix sound stage studio. Cary Grant later remembered talking to himself before the screen test, reminding himself of things he had learned at Astoria Studios making *Singapore Sue*. He told himself to relax, to look at the camera, to act naturally. He remembered Casey Robinson's directions to keep his right side towards the camera and to keep his chin up to diminish the size of his neck. He was determined to do well.

He ended up looking much better than the nervous Mrs Gering.

When the test was ready for viewing, there was good news and bad news. The bad news was that Mrs Gering didn't impress a single one of the studio executives who watched. The good news was that Archie Leach looked great.

Archie was staying at San Simeon. Within the week, he got a call there from B. P. Schulberg. Paramount offered the young Englishman a contract for five years plus options and a salary of $450 per week. (Coincidentally, this was the same amount Archie had asked the Shuberts for when he got back to New York from St Louis.) 'A standard deal,' Schulberg said. 'One other thing,' he added, 'if you accept, you'll have to change your name.'

Archie thought the offer over for a couple of days. He consulted with his friends who told him it was indeed a standard

deal for a newcomer and a good opportunity. Soon, he called
Schulberg and accepted the offer. He also called the Shuberts
to say he wouldn't be back.

Less than a month after arriving in California 'on vacation',
the man signed his first motion picture contract. He was told to
report for work after the Christmas holidays. Before he could
sign that contract, there was still the question of his name.
Archibald Alexander Leach had to go, but who was going to
replace him?

The birth of 'Cary Grant' took place in two stages. One night,
he was at dinner with Fay Wray and her husband, John Saunders. Wray suggested 'Cary Lockwood', which had been the
name of the character he had played opposite her in *Nikki*.

Archie thought it sounded all right. The next morning he
went to the studio to see Schulberg who always took a hand in
renaming the studio's new contract players. Schulberg had no
objections to 'Cary' but he already had an actor under contract
named Harold Lockwood, so that surname was out. What they
needed was a short, easy-to-remember last name like 'Cooper'
or 'Gable'. As Grant would always tell the story, 'A secretary
brought me a list and I simply closed my eyes and stuck a pin
into it and came up with "Grant".'

In fact, the decision was a little more studied than that.
Schulberg kept a list of short Anglo-Saxon surnames for just
this purpose. Archie slowly went through the list, studying
each potential name until he came to 'Grant'. He liked it, he
would say later, for 'no particular reason'. 'How about
"Grant"?' he asked Schulberg. The executive had no
objections.

Thus, undramatically, even off-handedly, Archie Leach
passed into oblivion at the age of 28 — and Cary Grant was
born. Gone was the impoverished, motherless boy from Bristol
who hung around backstage at music halls to find the light and
laughter he so sorely lacked at home. Perhaps in conscious
irony, soon after signing with Paramount, Cary Grant bought
himself a little dog he named 'Archie Leach'.

Cary Grant began his film career in the era of the big, important movie studios and the contract players whose lives they

ran. The studios paid their actors and actresses a lot of money and they kept them busy earning it.

Television was still a thing of the future. When the American public wanted to escape their humdrum daily lives, they went to the 'picture show' where there was always a happy ending, where they could vicariously enjoy the exciting, glamorous lives of their familiar heroes like Gary Cooper and Fredric March.

The demand was high and the competition was tough. The film factories turned out movie after movie, as fast as they could – usually in just a few short weeks. For example, Clark Gable appeared in eleven motion pictures in his first year with MGM. Cary Grant's first year at Paramount was also busy. He made a total of eight movies that year, including a money-maker that kept the financially faltering Paramount intact.

When Schulberg signed Grant, he thought he had the perfect part to launch the career of his newest find. Grant's first role was the second male lead opposite Thelma Todd and Lili Damita in *This Is the Night*, a bedroom farce. Grant plays an Olympic athlete married to Todd. His frequent travels give his wife time to pursue leading man Roland Young, who plays a Parisian bachelor. Grant comes home one night to find them together.

After a series of silly events, the three of them end up in Venice where Damita has been hired to play Young's wife. Conveniently, Grant falls in love with Damita, Todd and Young stay together, and in the best story-telling tradition, everyone lives happily ever after.

When he first saw the finished product, Grant cringed. He thought he was dreadful. How had he ever imagined that he could have a career in films? He was all set to pack up the Pack-ard for a fast drive back to Broadway and the Shuberts when Paramount executives convinced him that he was not all that bad. They were more than satisfied with his 'maiden voyage'.

He himself felt a little better when *Variety* reviewed the movie and said he was 'a potential femme rave'. Another reviewer wrote, 'I thought (Cary Grant) made a splendid figure.'

Long after he had become one of the world's leading movie stars, Grant loved to tell the story of one of the high points of his early days in Hollywood. It was the time he met the Great Garbo.

Around this time, he was living in Noel Coward's house. One day Coward called him at the studio: 'Come home quickly, dear boy, we're having Greta Garbo to tea.' As he later told the story, he was absolutely floored at the thought of meeting Garbo, then perhaps the world's biggest star. He just couldn't do it, he was simply too nervous. He fretted around the studio for hours and finally made his way home, thinking surely Garbo had left by then. But as he walked in the front door, she was on her way out. Summoning up the full measure of the Cary Grant charm, he shook her hand, looked her in the face, and stammered, 'I'm so happy you could meet me, Miss Garbo.'

Straight after *This Is the Night*, he was put to work on *Sinners in the Sun*, which starred Carole Lombard. He played a dashing gambler named Ridgeway. Grant's role was memorable only for the fact that it was the first time he appeared on screen in white tie and tails. As one critic aptly said, 'Young Grant looks like he was born in tails.' A good number of his future films would take advantage of that judgment and keep him in formal wear.

From there, Cary Grant next went to a small part in *Merrily We Go to Hell*, starring Fredric March and Sylvia Sidney. The two played a married couple with problems. March was a hard-drinking newspaperman who has written a play he fights hard to have produced on Broadway. Grant was the lead in the play when it finally reaches the stage. Grant's screen credit simply listed him as 'Stage Leading Man'. It was not a wonderful film.

There followed a fourth picture in which he had only the third male lead, but which oddly enough moved his career forward in a roundabout way.

It was the summer of 1932. Gary Cooper was without a doubt *the* big star on the Paramount lot. Warner had James Cagney and Errol Flynn; MGM had Clark Gable; and Paramount had 'Coop'. But he and Paramount head Adolph Zukor were feuding. Cooper had joined Paramount in 1927. By 1929, he had become its biggest box-office draw. Between 1929 and early 1931, he had made 19 films for the studio and was loudly complaining that he was being overworked. So, just about the same time that Cary Grant was being offered his first contract, Cooper left for Europe and Africa on an extended vacation.

Zukor was desperate to have Cooper back at work, but the star was playing hard to get. Finally, Zukor made him an offer unmatched in Hollywood in those days: the highest salary on the lot, the right to choose his films, and veto power over cast and directors.

Cooper returned in triumph to begin shooting *The Devil and the Deep* opposite Tallulah Bankhead. The film marked the American debut of British actor Charles Laughton. It was directed by Marion Gering who suggested that Grant, with his accent, would be perfect for a small role as a British Navy lieutenant who dies at the end of the first half-hour.

Not much can really be said about Grant's performance in *The Devil and the Deep*. All his role required of him was to stand around, look handsome and die at the appropriate moment. But more than one critic compared his looks very favourably with Cooper's, even if his role did not call for much acting ability.

The comparison was not lost on Schulberg, whose greatest fear was that Cooper was getting too big for his britches. He worried that Cooper might upset the smooth system that gave studio executives absolute control over even their major stars. He saw in Grant a way to show Cooper that even the biggest star was not indispensable.

The big project then on Paramount's drawing-board was to be the first film at the studio (their third in all) for Marlene Dietrich and her German-born director, Josef von Sternberg. It was a lavish production and Schulberg hoped it would be one of the year's box-office winners.

With considerable fanfare, Paramount announced that *Blonde Venus* would co-star the London stage actor, Herbert Marshall, in his American film debut – and Cary Grant. The movie was the story of a married woman who flatters a rich playboy to get the money needed to help her ailing husband. No one wanted the part of the playboy. Von Sternberg was known for ignoring male leads in favour of Dietrich. William Powell not only refused the role, but had a clause written into his contract that said he'd never have to work for the German. Gary Cooper had worked for him in *Morocco* and it was assumed he would do this picture. Instead, it went to Cary Grant.

Just about everyone in Hollywood saw the casting as a not-so-subtle message from Schulberg to Cooper. Everyone but Grant. It was his first starring role in a major film and he was determined to take advantage of the break no matter what the motivation for it.

Nothing in Gary Grant's short Hollywood career had prepared him for the circus that *Blonde Venus* became. Not long before shooting began, the Lindbergh kidnapping took place. Many Hollywood stars, including Marlene Dietrich, began to get threats of having their children kidnapped. She was a nervous wreck in the first weeks of filming and could barely work.

Then Schulberg and von Sternberg got into the kind of fight of which Hollywood legends are made. Schulberg wanted to end the film one way and von Sternberg another. Schulberg threw the director off the film and hired someone else. Von Sternberg went immediately to Berlin. Then Dietrich refused to work for any other director but von Sternberg and she, too, stormed off the set. Weeks of transatlantic negotiations followed. Meanwhile, the new director shot the scenes that didn't need Dietrich. Finally Schulberg and von Sternberg declared a truce, the director returned, and the film was finished.

Considering how it was made, there's little wonder that *Blonde Venus* opened to appalling reviews. The film might be best remembered for displaying Dietrich in an ape suit singing 'Hot Voodoo'. But, while more than one critic found the film 'disjointed', Cary Grant got the best reviews of his life. He won unanimous praise, with *The New York Times* noting: 'Cary Grant is worthy of a much better role than this.' Grant credited this movie with bringing him to the attention of Lowell Sherman, Mae West's director, which would later result in his first really important movie.

Schulberg read those reviews and agreed. He announced that Grant would star opposite Tallulah Bankhead in a major remake of *Blood and Sand* and then was embarrassed when she refused the project. He wanted to take advantage of Grant's momentum, but he didn't have anything immediately available. So he gave permission when Grant and the Western star Randolph Scott came to ask him if they could work together. The project became *Hot Saturday* and co-starred Grant, Scott and ingenue Nancy Carroll.

Grant and Scott had become the closest of friends and would remain so for years. At first, they shared an apartment and then later together rented a large house on West Live Oak Drive complete with a butler, a maid and a swimming-pool. It was soon to become a gathering spot for the 'in' young Hollywood crowd.

In *Hot Saturday* Grant played much the same role as he had in *Blonde Venus*, that of the suave young playboy who wins the girl from Scott, cast as the boyhood sweetheart. If his reviews in *Blonde Venus* were good, these were even better. *The New York Herald Tribune* called him 'A Gable-esque leading man . . . destined for screen popularity'. *Variety* called his performance 'well ahead of that of Miss Carroll or Mr Scott'. *Hot Saturday* was the first movie for which Cary Grant received top billing.

He was basking in the glow of this pleasant attention when his friend, Marion Gering, called. Gering was having trouble casting several roles for a film version of Puccini's *Madame Butterfly*. As a favour, would Cary play Lieutenant Pinkerton? Yes, as a favour to Gering, he would. His co-stars were Sylvia Sidney and Charlie Ruggles.

It was during the filming of *Madame Butterfly*, a film best forgotten, that he met Mae West and was cast in his first really big movie, *She Done Him Wrong*.

Two stories have been told about Cary Grant so often that people usually think they're true. Like most legends, the stories are a little fact and a lot of fiction. The first legend has to do with his dislike of telling his age, at least until he became an 'older' man. He even used to say he didn't know himself exactly how old he was because his birth certificate had been destroyed in a German Blitz. In fact, copies of all English birth certificates are kept safe in London, and his are in perfect condition. The legend has it that *Life* magazine was planning to use him as a cover story. They couldn't work out his exact age, so they wired, 'HOW OLD CARY GRANT?' The reply is said to have read, 'OLD CARY GRANT FINE. HOW YOU?'

It sounds like a perfect Cary Grant line, doesn't it? Unfortunately, he himself said it never happened, although he admitted that given such an opening, he hoped he would have replied like that.

The second legend has it that Cary Grant was 'discovered' by Mae West. Again, there's some truth to it, but not a lot. Mae West was a successful Broadway star who came to Hollywood in 1932 to make her second movie, *She Done Him Wrong*. There was no leading man cast for the picture. The legend goes that West was walking through the Paramount lot with her producer when she spied Cary Grant. She is then said to have turned to the producer and uttered one of her famous lines: 'He's gorgeous. If this one can talk, I'll take him.' Supposedly, this is how Cary Grant got his first movie role. Even Mae West said in her autobiography that she cast Grant after seeing him in the street.

The truth is, Cary Grant did appear with Mae West in *She Done Him Wrong*. It was his first successful film. West had indeed asked for him in the film. But in fact, it was the eighth film he made.

Grant, along with many other movie folk of the day, used to attend boxing matches regularly. He went to the Friday Night Fights at the American Legion Stadium in Hollywood with Randolph Scott. One night the two men ran into a group of people that included Mae West. A few days later, they met again on the Paramount lot. West asked director Lowell Sherman about him. Sherman had seen him and liked him, and between Sherman and West, Grant was cast in *She Done Him Wrong*.

Even though Mae West did not 'discover' Cary Grant, one

can't neglect the importance to his career of the two films with her, or the debt he owed her. He would later write: 'I owe everything to her. Well, not quite everything, but almost everything. She knows so much. Her instinct is so true, her timing so perfect, her grasp of the situation so right.' However, much later in his career he would become more honest about Mae West and what he thought of her, possibly in the face of her continued insistence that she had 'discovered' him.

'I don't have a fond memory of Mae West,' he came to admit. 'She had to control everything and did things her own way to the detriment of everyone around her. I think she wore so much make-up because of her own insecurity. I don't admire superficiality.'

In *She Done Him Wrong*, Grant played a policeman hunting a white slavery ring and posing as a Salvation Army officer. The mission he ran was next door to a saloon where the ring operated and at which the character played by West was performing. She was reprising her Broadway role as Diamond Lil. As was the Hollywood style of the 1930s, the two rehearsed for four days and then shot the Gay Nineties spoof in 16 days, from start to finish.

Grant's years in vaudeville as a straight man came to good use. His role in this film was to play the straight man, a morally upright lawman feeding lines to a woman of outrageous sexuality.

Half a dozen of her lines from the film have passed into common Hollywood use. Top of the list is the often misquoted 'Why don't you come up sometime and see me?' (It was not, 'Come up and see me sometime.') While looking Grant over from top to bottom, she said, 'Umm, warm, dark and handsome.' When he asked, 'Haven't you ever met a man who can make you happy?' she replied, 'Sure lots of times.'

Over the next six months, Cary Grant made three more pictures. *The Woman Accused*, a melodrama, was about a woman who kills her former lover, a villain, when he threatens her new beau, and their attempts to escape subsequent capture. This movie was released within ten days of *She Done Him Wrong*. Movie-goers were beginning to recognize Cary Grant, who was still in his first year of movie-making.

You may still see reruns of the next project, *The Eagle and the Hawk*, on television. This was a short (68 minutes) anti-war film with Cary Grant playing a pilot again. Fredric March was the hero, Carole Lombard was the girl. March, a veteran, has seen too much war. Lombard can't save him. He kills himself. Grant protects March's honour by making it seem as if he died in action, a hero.

Grant had been ordered to do *The Eagle and the Hawk* after Gary Cooper refused the film. Grant had begun to see himself as on a par with Cooper by this time, and resented the way he was being used. Justification of his position was all around. The critics loved him. The audience adored him. Bags of fan mail were arriving for him at the studio. Even more important, he could point to *She Done Him Wrong*.

Released in February, 1933, *She Done Him Wrong* was an instant hit. It eventually made a profit of over $2 million and saved the studio from bankruptcy. Paramount had been on the verge of selling its more than 1,700 theatres and merging with Metro-Goldwyn-Mayer. Neither move had to be made.

Paramount wanted West and Grant together again quickly, but West dragged her feet. The studio put Grant in an easily forgettable picture called *The Gambling Ship*. He played the familiar role of a bad man with a good heart, as a gangster on a cross-country train who falls in love with a girl who turns out to be on the run from her gangster ex-lover, the owner of a gambling ship. It was Grant's first top billing.

When Mae West and Cary Grant finally got together again, Paramount's gratitude went to West. For the next picture, *I'm No Angel*, they paid her the enormous sum of $300,000. Cary Grant was not completely forgotten. He got a rise – to $750 a week. It was his twelfth movie.

I'm No Angel did even better at the box office than *She Done Him Wrong*. In it, West delivered another immortal line to Grant, 'When I'm good, I'm very good . . . but when I'm bad, I'm better.' She played a circus sideshow vamp who ends up falling for the naïve but ostentatious Cary Grant. After suing him for breach of promise, she at last wins his heart.

Not only was *I'm No Angel* a financial success, it also won good reviews for Grant. *Variety* said, 'Nice work'. Another critic said that casting him had been 'a brilliant piece of dramatic awareness. He is perfect in the role.'

A now familiar scenario was developing. Grant, with Mae West, had made two of Paramount's highest grossing hits at the box office – within six months of each other. Even his three pictures in between had been well received. The public and the critics liked him. He felt he deserved more money and was very angry with the studio. He didn't think he was appreciated. The studio, on the other hand, felt he was not properly grateful for his rise.

The year 1934, when Cary Grant was 30 years old, was not a happy one for him, professionally or personally. He had a brief, failed marriage with a woman named Virginia Cherrill.

Virginia Cherrill had come to Hollywood in 1928 from Chicago after a short marriage there to a lawyer named Irving Adler. A society girl with no acting experience, she had to rely on her extraordinary good looks. These looks, including blue eyes and blonde hair, got her several screen tests when she arrived. She did not, however, get work. With not much else to do, she became a regular on the Hollywood party circuit.

One night in 1930, she was at the popular Friday Night Fights. Charlie Chaplin saw her there and immediately wanted her for a part he had been unable to fill. She was to play the blind flower-girl in his silent film classic, *City Lights*.

Chaplin had looked at a lot of actresses before he found Virginia. He gave her a screen test and on that basis, cast her in one of Hollywood's most famous debuts. He later said, 'She somehow had the knack of playing a blind person.'

After *City Lights*, Virginia signed with 20th Century-Fox which used her only in minor roles. Her incredible looks continued to draw attention. Louella Parsons called her 'Hollywood's greatest beauty'. She kept her connections with high society, and for a short time was seen in the company of William Rhinelander Stewart, a New York millionaire and one of the most eligible men in America.

Cary Grant and Virginia Cherrill first met at that famous meeting spot, the Friday Night Fights. Later, he ran into her

again in the Paramount commissary. She was on loan from
Fox for a small part. They chatted and it was love at first (well,
second) sight. Actually, a little second sight might have saved
them from what was to be a very painful relationship. They
began going out together, to the delight of the gossip
columnists. They continued to date during 1933.

Having made twelve movies in less than two years, Grant
wanted to take some time off after *I'm No Angel*, but Adolph
Zukor, Paramount's president, called. He was trying to finish a
version of *Alice in Wonderland* in time to get it into Radio City
Music Hall for Christmas. Scheduled to feature the famous
Bing Crosby, the 'crooner' was forced to bow out after shooting had already started. Zukor called Cary Grant, who filled in.

Alice only needed a couple of weeks' work, so when it was
finished, Grant at last took his holiday. He and Virginia went to
Arizona. They were forced to cut the vacation short when
reporters found them. There had been rumours that they had
run away to get married. As the two of them departed hastily to
catch a plane home, Grant angrily told the press, 'We are not
going to marry.'

Virginia went off to England to be in a movie. In the case of
Cary and Virginia, the old saying 'Absence makes the heart
grow fonder' seemed to hold true. Grant started thinking of
marriage. Also, it had been a very long time since he had seen
either of his parents. In what's described as almost a whim, he
and his friend, Randy Scott, set off for England.

In November, 1933, Cary Grant arrived in Bristol in the
classic role of 'Local Boy Makes Good'. The poor factory
worker's son was now an American Movie Star. He had not
seen his father in the 13 years since he had embarked for
America on the *Olympic*, and it had been 20 years since he had
last seen his mother.

He and Elias had a happy reunion. There was a family party
where he was re-introduced to relatives he didn't remember
meeting in the first place. He took Randy Scott on a tour of
Fairfield where the new headmaster seemed almost as glad to
see him arrive as old Gussie Smith had been to see him leave.

Elias asked his son a question that was difficult for both of them. Would he be going to see his mother who was still at the Fishponds institution? Cary had thought about it before he came. Yes, he would go to see her. Elsie's birthday was February 8 – she would be 57 – and he would visit her then.

After the visit to Bristol, it was back to London where Cary stayed with Virginia. In early December, he entered a clinic for surgery to repair some damage he'd suffered on a movie set. The previous March, during the filming of *The Eagle and the Hawk*, he had been standing next to a bomb that prematurely exploded.

Just before Christmas, the couple went to Bristol, where he introduced one and all to 'Ginny', and threw a party for family and friends at the Bristol Grand Hotel.

All during January, Cary stayed in London with Virginia. He had to be back in California by the middle of February to start a new film. His plans were to visit his mother on February 8 and then leave immediately for America. Passage had already been booked for Virginia and him on the liner *Paris*.

The question was first whether to get married, and if so, when and where. He agonized over the decision. Whether he really wanted to get married or whether it was simply a case of bowing to the growing pressure is not really clear, but during his stay in the clinic, he decided to go ahead and do it. Then he could not decide whether to marry in England or wait until they were back in California. He thought about getting married among his family and friends in Bristol, but that would have meant a planned wedding, previously announced, and a full-blown circus, courtesy of the press. That option was scrapped. Cary and Virginia even toyed with the idea of being married by the captain at sea aboard the *Paris* on the way home. Then they learned that, all those romantic stories to the contrary, such a marriage would not be considered legal in California.

That reduced the options to marrying in England or waiting until they got back to California. To reserve the possibility of a London wedding, the legally required notice of the marriage was formally announced. This set off the press. They besieged the couple, demanding to know when the two would be married. Cary and Virginia still could not decide.

On February 8, Cary Grant at last had his reunion with his mother. Despite any qualms he may have had, it turned out to be easy. Elsie acted as though twenty minutes and not twenty years had passed since that day he had come home from school to find her gone. He was still her little Archie. Elsie knew about his movie career from her relatives. They read about it from time to time in the Bristol newspapers. Now he told her about his life in America and his plans for the future, including his forthcoming marriage. Twenty years had gone by, but now the two would remain close for the rest of Elsie's long life.

The next day dawned bright and clear. Cary and Virginia were due to catch the boat train for Plymouth early in the afternoon. Suddenly, he decided that they should get married that morning, timing it so that they would go directly from the ceremony to the train. Virginia would say later that he gave her fifteen minutes' notice.

Cary Grant, heart-throb of millions, and Virginia Cherrill, one of the most beautiful women in the world, were married at the Caxton Hall Registry Office in Westminster on February 9, 1934. The ceremony was brief. In England, he was legally still old Archie, so Virginia became Mrs Leach. The two emerged to a sea of clamouring reporters and photographers. He only managed to shout, 'We're very happy,' before ducking into the waiting cab and being driven hastily to the station.

Back in Hollywood, life may have been a bed of roses, but only if you're referring to the thorns. Grant continued to be terribly unhappy with Paramount and the unhappiness carried over into his home-life. Virginia had 'retired' from show business upon her marriage to him.

Unhappy or not, Grant kept working. Within the first three months of being back in Hollywood, Paramount put him in three movies in quick succession. He thought they were all dreadful. It seemed to him that the studio had no real idea how to use him, since the movies were a romantic comedy, an adventure and a straight romance.

One film, *Born to Be Bad*, looked as if it might have been a hit when it first got under way. Darryl F. Zanuck had just left Warner Brothers where he had made the highly successful movie, *The Public Enemy*, with Jimmy Cagney. He was now with 20th Century-Fox and wanted another project with equal shock value.

Born to Be Bad was the story of a promiscuous woman of few scruples with a somewhat delinquent son. Loretta Young got the part. She and her son stage a phony car accident whose victim is a wealthy, rather timid businessman. The woman falls in love with him and he, in turn, manages to reform both mother and son.

Zanuck's challenge was to find the right leading man for Loretta Young and then to develop, on screen, a steamy relationship between the two that will ultimately change them both. Zanuck wanted Cary Grant (mostly for his looks, he would later admit) and so he went to Adolph Zukor of Paramount. Zukor agreed to give him Grant, but charged an enormous fee for the service.

Then came a major hitch. On July 1, 1934, the 'Production Code' was put into strict effect. The Hays Office, a self-regulatory organization within the film industry, developed the Code to counter Hollywood scandals and promote a sense of wholesomeness. What it amounted to was censorship.* *Born to Be Bad* was one of the first scripts submitted for this review.

The same script did not come back. Many scenes had to be completely rewritten. The film had lost much of its reason for being. Zanuck had already spend a lot of money on it,

---

* Also known as the Hays Code and remaining in effect until 1966, the Code set forth standards of 'good taste' and specific do's and don't's. Among some of its rules: 'The sympathy of the audience should never be thrown to the side of crime, wrongdoing, evil or sin; ministers of religion . . . should not be used as comic characters or villains; excessive and lustful kissing, lustful embracing, suggestive postures and gestures, are not to be shown; miscegenation (sex between blacks and whites) is forbidden; pointed profanity (this includes the words God, Lord, Jesus, Christ – unless used reverently – Hell, S.O.B., damn, Gawd), or other profane or vulgar expressions, however used, is forbidden.' Violence got off easier than sex: 'Actual hanging or electrocutions . . . brutality and possibly gruesomeness . . . (should) be treated within the careful limits of good taste.'

especially to Zukor for Cary Grant, so he went ahead with the now anaemic script. It was a disaster at the box office and was soon forgotten.

Darryl Zanuck was disturbed by the whole project for a long time. As Cary Grant went on to be such a master of light comedy, Zanuck realized he should have given up the drama in *Born to Be Bad* and allowed Cary Grant to play his scenes for laughs, not emotion. It might have saved the picture.

Grant's other two pictures in this period were *Thirty-Day Princess*, directed by Marion Gering, with Sylvia Sidney as a stand-in for an ailing princess on a goodwill tour of the US; and *Kiss and Make Up*, a fully forgettable film with Grant playing a beautician opposite Helen Mack and wearing a lot of formal attire.

In those days, major studios kept what amounted to a 'B' team to play the parts their top stars turned down. Critic Richard Schickel points out that from 1934 to 1935, Cary Grant was clearly Paramount's 'second-string Gary Cooper'. Grant had realized this and he didn't like it. Even more irritating was what happened next.

All Hollywood was talking about the young Irving Thalberg's* intention to mount a major new film based on a new book called *Mutiny on the Bounty*. From the moment it was announced, *Mutiny on the Bounty* was destined to be the film of the year.

---

* Irving Thalberg's life story would make a good movie itself. Becoming Universal studio's head of production at 20, he was the first person ever to be called 'The Boy Wonder'. The name came from the title of a *Saturday Evening Post* story by a former Universal writer, about a producer said to be modelled on Thalberg. He moved to MGM, making that studio the most prestigious and glamorous one in Hollywood by the early 1930s. He instituted the now standard 'sneak preview'. In 1932, he had a heart attack at the age of 33. After recovering, he made such great films as *Mutiny on the Bounty*, *A Night at the Opera* and *The Good Earth*. After he succumbed to pneumonia at the age of 37, the Academy of Motion Picture Arts and Sciences established the Irving G. Thalberg Award, given ever since 'for the most consistent high level of production achievement by an individual producer'.

Clark Gable was already signed to play the lead in this MGM picture, and Thalberg was looking for men for the two second leads. He called Grant, who immediately agreed to take one of the roles, assuming, of course, that Paramount would lend him to MGM. Schulberg said he had no objections, realizing the role would boost Grant's career which would make him a more valuable property to Paramount. But he said it was a decision that had to be made by studio head Adolph Zukor, and so passed the request to him.

Zukor was still smarting over the hard bargain that MGM had driven when it seemed, before the Mae West films, that Paramount was going to fold. He turned Thalberg's request down cold, saying that Grant was simply too busy and too valuable to be lent out.

Franchot Tone accepted the role denied to Grant. *Mutiny on the Bounty* went on to be the year's top grossing film. It won the Academy Award for Best Picture and each of its male leads, Clark Gable, Charles Laughton and Franchot Tone, were nominated for Best Actor.

In the meantime, Zukor assigned Grant to star opposite opera diva Elissa Landi in a quickly forgotten effort called *Enter Madame*. Grant's principal function in the film was again to dress in formal clothes and look handsome. He was playing Landi's long-suffering husband in this light romantic comedy. Ironically, Grant received some of his better reviews for this picture – not because he had much of a role, but because he made the most of it.

Cary Grant never forgave Zukor for not allowing him to work for Thalberg. Their relationship went steadily downhill. At one point, Zukor was so angry with Grant that he forced him to accept a loan-out to MGM for a second-rate project. On the day *Mutiny on the Bounty* received its Academy Award, Cary Grant was at MGM working on *Suzy*, another soon forgotten World War I flying-ace movie. Apparently it was okay to lend him to MGM just so long as the movie looked unpromising. (*Suzy* was a romantic tragedy also starring Jean Harlow.)

Cary and Virginia continued to have serious difficulties with their marriage. She went home to her mother several times. He always went after her and brought her back. He attributed their problems to his bringing home his unhappiness with the studio. Finally, in November of 1934, Virginia filed for divorce. The public hearings were messy. A settlement was at last achieved and the divorce was granted in March 1935.

Virginia went back to England to act again. She was to remarry three more times. One of her husbands was the ninth Earl of Jersey to whom she was married from 1937 to 1946.

Angry as he was, Grant continued to make films throughout 1934 and 1935:

Ladies Should Listen, a so-so farce in which Grant played a rich, misunderstood businessman whose life was manipulated by a telephone operator, played by Frances Drake. Again, Grant received good reviews for his own performance, being compared to *the* Movie Star of the day, Clark Gable. One critic wrote, 'I was particularly pleased with Cary Grant. Like Clark Gable in *It Happened One Night*, he surprises everyone with his delightful flair for light comedy.'

Wings in the Dark, for which he received good reviews as a pilot and inventor blinded by a gas explosion. Myrna Loy played the love interest as a sky-writing stunt flier.

The Last Outpost, an easily forgettable action-adventure picture about British troops in Africa, with Grant being captured by Kurds in the desert. His co-stars included Claude Rains.

As 1936 came up on the calendar, Cary Grant was exhausted. He had had a short, unhappy marriage followed by a bitter divorce. He had made several movies he disliked. He thought his studio was taking advantage of him as well as stymying his career. Not only was he tired, he was angry and ready to leave Paramount. He never wanted to be bound to a single studio again.

5

GOING IT ALONE

Sylvia Scarlett was filmed in 1935 and released in 1936. The off-beat story of a ne'er-do-well and his daughter who take to the road when he gets into trouble, the film featured Katharine Hepburn as the daughter who disguises herself as a boy as they tour the countryside. Edmund Gwenn played the embezzling father. Their travelling companion was Cary Grant as a Cockney con-man they meet along the way.

If there was a single turning point in Cary Grant's film career, it was the making of *Sylvia Scarlett*. The film is an adaptation of a book, *The Early Life and Adventures of Sylvia Scarlett*, and was a pet project of the young Hepburn. Grant got this pivotal role because of her.

Cary Grant was once asked who, of all his leading ladies, was his favourite. He thought for a minute and then admitted it was probably Grace Kelly. 'She was not only astonishingly beautiful, but she also possessed that incredible serenity. Yet when she was in a scene with you, she was really with you, because while she was such a likeable and fun person, she would really listen.' Then he was asked who was his best co-star. His answer was immediate. 'Katharine Hepburn,' he confided, 'because of her professionalism, her courage and because she was foolish enough to trust me.'

The story of how the film made it to the screen, of how Cary Grant came to be its co-star, is one of a strange mixture of old and new friendships. Coming from a wealthy family, Hepburn became a stage actress after college. Her up-and-down stage

77

career mirrored her film career in many ways. She made a poor start, getting fired on several occasions; but in 1932, she became an almost overnight sensation in the *Warrior's Husband* on Broadway. She made several screen tests for different studios, but no one liked what they saw.

George Cukor had come to Hollywood from Broadway in 1929, starting at Universal as a dialogue director. (It was the beginning of 'talkies' and Broadway experience was very helpful.) His first picture was *All Quiet on the Western Front*. His first solo directing job was *Tarnished Lady*, Tallulah Bankhead's movie debut, for Paramount Publix. He was soon fired from that studio and followed his friend David O. Selznick to RKO (and later to MGM). Later he would direct such classics as *Camille* with Greta Garbo, *The Philadelphia Story*, *A Star Is Born* with Judy Holliday, and *My Fair Lady* for which he won an Academy Award.

In 1932, Cukor was looking for a young actress to play the daughter of John Barrymore in *A Bill of Divorcement*, a film he was about to make for RKO. He was going through a collection of old screen tests when he ran across one of Hepburn's. He liked her immediately, remembering her from Broadway. Cukor insisted that RKO bring her to Hollywood for the part. They were not immediately convinced, but finally on the basis of her Broadway hit, agreed to bring her out for the one film. They refused to give her a contract.

Filming started. Everyone on the set knew she was a sensation. The role fitted her perfectly. RKO offered her a five-year contract after seeing only the rushes from the first week's shooting.

Many Hollywood historians consider Katharine Hepburn's performance in *A Bill of Divorcement* as the single most significant debut in movie history. She followed that up by an inspired performance in her third film, *Morning Glory*, in which she played a young actress. *Morning Glory* won her an Oscar for Best Actress. She went on to give a solid performance for Cukor again in *Little Women*, which Cukor always called his best film.

Then, suddenly, her career took a quick turn downward.

She had a couple of misses, and showed some bad judgment by refusing the role of Joan of Arc. Finally, director George Stevens rescued her with the movie *Alice Adams*. Critics loved it, and audiences flocked to the cinemas. This renewed RKO's faith in her. As part of a new contract, they gave her the right to choose her own scripts.

The movie she wanted to make was based on the *Sylvia Scarlett* book she had read some years earlier. At the time, it was considered daring, since it made heroes out of con-men, and, in the first half of the film, the heroine has all her hair cut off and dresses as a boy.

Several studios had already passed on the project. The word around town was that it did not have much of a chance to succeed. Finally, Hepburn recruited Cukor and together they persuaded RKO to do the picture. RKO's motivation was to keep Hepburn and Cukor happy, rather than any real high hopes for the script.

The next person to get involved in the saga was, of all people, Howard Hughes. He and Hepburn were romantically involved at the time. Coincidentally, Hughes later bought RKO. The young millionaire and aeroplane inventor had been a close friend of Cary Grant's almost from the day the actor arrived in Hollywood. Hughes and Grant had been men about town together and Hughes knew how badly Grant felt about his failed marriage to Virginia Cherrill.

Hughes suggested to Hepburn that Grant would be perfect for the male lead in *Sylvia Scarlett*. Hepburn, in turn, discussed it with Cukor who was at first reluctant but then agreed. Together, Hepburn and Cukor took the idea to the film's producer, Pandro S. Berman.

Berman, at that time, was producing a film starring Grant's best friend and (again) roommate, Randolph Scott. Berman had agreed to take Scott on loan-out from Paramount as a favour to Adolph Zukor. (Zukor didn't have any work for Scott at the time, but was obligated to pay him anyway.) Scott naturally endorsed Grant. Berman agreed to ask Paramount to lend Grant for the picture. He didn't think there'd be much difficulty since Zukor owed him a favour for taking Scott. He also knew that Paramount was unhappy with Grant's attitude. What's more, no one expected *Sylvia Scarlett* to do very well.

Paramount made no difficulties and Grant went to work with Katharine Hepburn. He was paid $15,000 to do the picture. While that was far below the $50,000 Hepburn got, it was nonetheless the most he had ever made for a single project.

Grant and Hepburn hit it off immediately. He later wrote: 'She was a slip of a woman and I never really liked skinny women. But she had this thing, this air you might call it, the most totally magnetic woman I'd ever seen, and probably have ever seen since.'

Just as so many had predicted, *Sylvia Scarlett* was a disaster. Pandro Berman himself would eventually call it 'one of the worst pictures ever made'. The critics burned it. The audiences stayed away in droves. Nowadays, it's shown in nostalgia theatres and on television because of the love audiences maintain for those two movie stars it showcases.

Cukor recalled *Sylvia Scarlett*'s preview: 'It was awful. People were running up the aisles. Kate went into the ladies' room and found a woman lying down. She asked her if the picture was that bad, and the woman just rolled her eyes. Then we met Pandro Berman later in the evening and asked him to simply scrap the film, that we would do another for him for free. He refused but said, "I never want to see either of you ever again," and he wasn't kidding. It wasn't very pleasant.'

No one, neither audience nor critic, could really understand the story. None of it was made any easier by the fact that Hepburn spent so much of the film dressed as a man. Nor was it helped by the dialogue. On one occasion, the second male lead, Brian Aherne, had to say, 'There's something queer' about the fact that he felt strangely attracted to the 'young boy' played, of course, by Hepburn. It was not drama. It was not comedy. It was meant to be a sort of tragi-comedy, but it was neither funny nor tragic. In the reviews, several critics said it seemed that many in the cast were acting in different movies.

Cukor was once asked if he and the cast knew how bad the movie would be during the filming. 'Oh, no,' he replied, 'but Kate said afterward that about halfway through she began losing confidence in the material. She thought I was, also, but she never asked me or said anything about it. I found certain scenes very difficult to do, though. When they don't play themselves, to use the old cliché, it's very worrying. A good scene somehow falls into place and carries itself. These didn't.'

In later years, Cukor said that, as far as he was concerned, the single funniest thing he had ever experienced in his long Hollywood career was that a film as awful as *Sylvia Scarlett* ended up having something of a cult following. But while the movie itself was ghastly, Cary Grant's reviews were practically ecstatic.

Variety raved, 'Grant steals the picture.' The *Herald* said, 'Grant's is far the best performance.' *Time* concurred, 'Cary Grant's superb depiction of the Cockney steals the show.' The *New York Times* said, 'Cary Grant, whose previous work has too often been that of a charm merchant, turns actor in the role of the unpleasant Cockney and is surprisingly good at it.'

The strange thing that had happened was that under the steady direction of Cukor, and opposite Hepburn, Grant, as Cukor later put it, 'suddenly burst into bloom'. 'Up until then,' Cukor said, 'Cary had been a conventional leading man. He knew this raffish kind of life. He had been a stilt-walker in a circus. Suddenly this part hit him and he felt the ground under his feet. I think he gave a remarkable performance.'

Much of the credit for this phenomenon can be given to director George Cukor. Always one of Hepburn's favourites, Cukor was known as an 'actor's director'. Many stereotyped him further as a 'woman's director'. The performances he was able to elicit from so many brilliant actresses seem to justify the label. Most of them will admit he was able to bring out the best of their talent. In addition to Hepburn, he made terrific movies with Norma Shearer and Joan Crawford. Cukor guided Greta Garbo through her finest screen performance in *Camille*.

His skills were truly not limited to actresses. Under his direction, Cary Grant found his screen personality. He developed that light touch of comedy that was to carry him successfully through nearly all of his subsequent roles and was to earn him untold fans. Of this experience, Grant later said,

'For once they didn't see me as just a pleasant young man with black hair, white teeth and a heart of gold.' Cary Grant was suddenly recognized as a talent, and for the first time, began to believe himself that he could be an actor.

During the shooting of *Sylvia Scarlett*, Grant learned that his father's health was failing. He wished to go home to England and spend some time with him. Providentially, he was asked to star in a film called *The Amazing Quest of Ernest Bliss*. The picture was going to be made at Elstree Studios close to London. When he finished *Sylvia Scarlett*, Paramount did not have another project immediately ready. *Sylvia* hadn't been released so the raves for Grant were not yet in. Paramount agreed to let him go to England. He left in early November, 1935.

The movie was a remake of a silent classic in which a rich young man who has never worked a day in his life bets that he can live for a year on what he actually earns, without resorting to his great wealth. He loses the bet when his new-found lady love announces she must forsake him to marry her rich, but nasty, boss in order to get money for her sister's operation.

Elias Leach died one week after filming began on *Ernest Bliss*. He was 63 years old. His son was there for the funeral. He stood by the graveside in the Bristol churchyard to say goodbye to the man he'd seen so briefly since he'd become an adult. In his eulogy, Archie Leach/Cary Grant said of his father, 'He was a wise and kindly man, and I loved him very much.'

Mrs Leach had finally been released from Fishponds and was living back in Bristol. Since his short visit when she was still confined, they had kept in touch with an occasional letter or cable.

Following Elias Leach's funeral, Grant brought Elsie to London with him while he completed filming *Ernest Bliss*. He wanted her to move back to California with him, but when he asked her, she said no. In deference to her wishes, Grant took her back to Bristol when the shooting was finished. There, he placed her in a comfortable house not far from her brothers who would keep an eye on her and help her out as needed. Grant's work in England concluded with another quickie movie which had two alternative titles, *Romance and Riches* and

Amazing Adventure, whereupon he returned to California.

He greeted Hollywood with fresh enthusiasm. This was the first time he had been back in California since the release of *Sylvia Scarlett* and the superb reviews he had achieved. Also, while saddened by his father's death, he was at the same time very pleased to have a relationship with his mother again. Even though she refused to leave Bristol, she was well and was clearly back in his life to stay.

He expected to be able to reap the benefits of *Sylvia Scarlett*, but Paramount did not come through. Instead of being propelled ahead, he was shuttled into a series of forgettable projects. The first of his 1936 releases was a picture called *Big Brown Eyes*, a romantic mystery. His co-stars were Joan Bennett, Walter Pidgeon and Lloyd Nolan. Cary Grant played a rough and tough wisecracker with a good heart. He quits his job as a New York City cop to protest the release of a child murderer who gains his freedom through political connections. He and Joan Bennett, as a reporter, go on to solve crimes.

He was clearly ill-suited for this role and it showed in his performance. When he was called upon to play the tough guy on screen, he seemed like a fish out of water. A reviewer noted: 'One disappointment was the work of Cary Grant, who seemed ill at ease as the two-fisted detective. Grant has turned in one capable performance after another. In this one, he somehow didn't click. Perhaps it is that his innate good breeding subconsciously rebels against the role of a good-natured plebeian.' The film itself could not decide what it wanted to be: a suspense drama or a wacky comedy. Even before filming was finished, Grant was complaining long and loud to Paramount executives.

Paramount's response was to lend him to MGM for *Suzy*. Once again he was cast in the now familiar role of a World War I flying hero. He was supposed to be French; Jean Harlow's showgirl was American; and the Frenchman, Franchot Tone, played a British spy married to Harlow – in wartime Britain. Thinking Tone has been killed, Harlow goes to Paris after the war and marries Grant. However, Tone is not dead and appears in Paris where he is then killed in a spy plot. Harlow and Grant must then make it look as if he actually did die in the war before they were married, so they can live happily ever after.

The word around town was the project was in trouble. Rumour had it that the script had undergone numerous rewrites by three different screenwriters. Grant later found out it had actually been totally rewritten by four different writers. The producers could not decide how to portray the Harlow character – as an innocent or as highly sexual. Grant looked particularly uncomfortable playing a Frenchman: he couldn't do the accent. The Frenchman Tone played an Englishman oddly.

Grant's mood was not improved when, early in the filming, the entire MGM lot began to celebrate its Academy Award victory for *Mutiny on the Bounty*, the film that Paramount had refused to let him make.

Surprisingly, all three of *Suzy*'s stars got great reviews, although the movie itself didn't. Grant's reviews were especially good. One major Hollywood critic said, 'Cary Grant is something more than just a leading man. Since his outstanding performance in *Sylvia Scarlett*, his talents for varied characterizations have been recognized, and in each new venture he makes good. In this role he does full justice.'

By now *Ernest Bliss* had opened in London to excellent reviews. *The Times* wrote, Mr Cary Grant moves things along with a smooth and tactful performance.' Another reviewer noted, 'Cary Grant looks and acts the part with deft characterization. He secures laughs easily and without apparent effort.'

Given the combination of good reviews, Grant once again expected Paramount to recognize his talents and to cast him in bigger and better roles. But again he was disappointed.

After *Suzy*, the studio put him opposite his *Big Brown Eyes* co-star, Joan Bennett, in a picture called *Wedding Present*. In this forgettable outing, Grant played a crazy newspaperman, promoted into management against his will. He botches everything up, and loses the love and respect of his girl, Bennett, a former fellow reporter. She decides to marry someone else, but Grant arrives at her door with a 'wedding present', a fleet of emergency vehicles (she loves anything with a siren). He carries her off in an ambulance marked 'Insane Asylum'.

Again, it was a wooden performance by an actor who felt totally wrong for the part. He looked especially uncomfortable in the final scenes in the asylum wagon. The best review he got called his performance 'lackadaisical'. It was perfectly obvious that Paramount still considered Cary Grant to be part of its second string of leading men.

He had now been with the studio for close to the entire five years of his original contract. He had made over 20 pictures. Among them, *She Done Him Wrong* had saved the financially strapped Paramount. *Sylvia Scarlett*, although filmed on loan to RKO, had established his acting credentials beyond a doubt. Yet Cary Grant did not feel appreciated by his studio. As Rodney Dangerfield might say, 'He didn't get no respect.'

The time had come to renegotiate the contract. Paramount offered to renew for $2,500 a week, a proposal they considered extremely generous. In fact, it was no small piece of change – until you considered the box-office (i.e. dollars) appeal he had. Cary Grant countered with a demand that he be treated the same way other major stars were. He wanted the right to choose his own projects and to turn down any role he did not like. The studio refused immediately. On the Paramount lot, only Mae West, Gary Cooper and Marlene Dietrich had this privilege. They did not think Grant was in this league. They would give him more money, but not script and project approval.

As the negotiations dragged on, Grant found a project that he thought would move him into new areas and help his career. Robert Riskin had written Frank Capra's two monster hits, *It Happened One Night* and *Mr Deeds Goes to Town*, movies that made stars of Gary Cooper and Clark Gable. Lately, Riskin had written a musical called *When You're in Love* for Harry Cohn at Columbia. Grant asked to be loaned out to Columbia for the project. Paramount executives, who were unhappy with his contract demands, quickly agreed.

When You're in Love was the story of an Australian singer in Mexico, played by opera star Grace Moore, who needs to find a quick American husband in order to get into the US to sing at a big music festival. The accommodating man is Cary Grant, who plays a wealthy, wandering artist who meets Moore in a bar in a Mexican border town. As might be expected, Moore ends up falling in love with her husband. Cohn allowed Riskin to direct and he was not up to the job. The film did have a certain charm, but Riskin mostly let it be a showcase for Moore. Once again Grant played a window-dressing role. The film was by no means a disaster, but it was quickly forgotten.

Next came what Grant thought was a stroke of luck. RKO had been planning a lavish production, *The Toast of New York*, a biographical drama about Wall Street pioneer, Jim Fisk. The story, basically a love triangle, was slated to star Edward Arnold as Fisk, William Powell as his partner, and Ginger Rogers as the love interest. First Powell and then Rogers became unavailable. RKO signed Frances Farmer to fill the female lead, and asked Paramount for Grant to fill the role originally planned for Bill Powell. Paramount, still annoyed about the contract negotiations, agreed.

On paper it looked like a dream role. At the end of the movie, Fisk was to die and Grant to get the girl. Unfortunately, the film didn't work out. The script was taken from two different books and had been worked on, at one time or another, by six different writers. The final shooting script was a series of poor compromises between various previous versions. The Hays Office censors didn't help.

Frances Farmer, the leading lady, suffered from alcoholism and emotional problems. She would later be institutionalized for many years. At the time of *The Toast of New York*, her frequent outbursts caused a great deal of turmoil on the set. Between the script problems and Farmer, the final product was a muddle and a disaster at the box office. RKO lost over $500,000 on the movie, a considerable sum in those days.

Grant was still in contract negotiations with Paramount. He faced a dilemma. He couldn't bear playing any more parts that could eventually hurt his career and his popularity by their inferiority. The studio wouldn't give in. It was the age of studios. No one had worked freelance since the 1920s.

Frank Vincent became Cary Grant's new agent, and later his

manager and lifelong friend. Vincent firmly believed that Grant was good enough and popular enough to make it on his own. He convinced his client of this. It was a tough decision, similar to the one Grant had to make when he turned down a long-term contract with the Shuberts in favour of a run-of-the-play agreement.

Taking Vincent's advice, Grant paid $11,800 to buy out the remaining time on his Paramount contract. With that, he vowed he would never tie himself to a single studio again.

At the beginning of 1937, Cary Grant was at last on his own. The world was conspiring in his favour. The Depression was basically over. People were flocking to the movie theatres. Movie studios that had wondered how they were going to make ends meet now had so much money they were hard-pressed to spend it. It seemed Grant's career timing was as good as his timing before the camera.

In 1937 alone, the studios produced 778 feature films. Every actor was in demand, even one like Cary Grant who had eschewed a studio contract. America's 18,000 cinemas were full. Some sound stages were booked for double shifts – a day shoot for one movie, a night shoot for another. Tastes in movies were also changing. Comedies were becoming lighter. Leading ladies were portraying more independent women. Kate Hepburn and Bette Davis were prime examples. Screen courtships were a little less romantic and much wittier (perhaps a positive by-product of the Hays Code). William Powell and Myrna Loy as detectives Nick and Nora Charles in the series that began with Dashiell Hammett's *The Thin Man* were the epitome of this trend.

In other words, movies were going just the right way to fit the image Cary Grant wanted to project: the charming, witty, perennial bachelor, desired by every woman but attainable by none. Striking out on his own was the best thing he could have done.

Nevertheless, Grant did not get off to a flying start. Finally able to make his own decisions, he found himself unsure of just what he wanted to do. His life was his own. Gone were the studio executives who could be cajoled, argued with, begged from and cursed at, and who ultimately made all the choices. It was up to him now.

He would later write of the period, 'I suddenly became aware that I wasn't sure what or who I was on the screen. As an actor I had a thin veneer of sophistication carefully copied from Noel Coward. I'd casually put my hand in my pocket and it would get stuck there from perspiration.'

What should he do? Should he look for a role that demanded acting, like *Sylvia Scarlett*, or just concentrate on roles that demanded debonair good looks, like *Blonde Venus*?

He decided to look not so much at scripts, but at directors and actors and actresses with whom he'd like to work. This led him to the famous, highly respected Henry Hathaway. Hathaway's latest project was a picture called *Spawn of the North*, slated to star Grant's friends Randy Scott and Carole Lombard. Hathaway was known for his Westerns, often starring Scott.

After his divorce, Grant had moved back in with Randy Scott in Scott's house on the beach at Malibu. The two were as compatible as ever, but clearly needed more room. Grant liked the idea of living at the beach but did not enjoy the long daily drive from Malibu into the city.

The area near the beach at Santa Monica was becoming very fashionable. Among the magnificent homes there was one owned by actress Norma Talmadge. It had seven bedrooms, a private screening room, and a huge pool. It also had a stunning, uninterrupted view of the ocean. After a little haggling, Talmadge agreed to sell it to Grant and Scott. The two made a pledge. Whoever married first could buy the other out.

Grant got his wish with director Henry Hathaway. At Scott's urging, Hathaway agreed to cast Grant as the second male lead in *Spawn of the North*. The picture was scheduled to go on location to Alaska for some of the scenes. This was unusual in those days. Grant was looking forward to it.

Unfortunately, Carole Lombard came down with influenza and had to be replaced. The role was taken over by Dorothy Lamour. Hathaway didn't think either Grant or Scott were right with Lamour. Their roles were filled by Henry Fonda and George Raft respectively. This left Cary Grant with little to do but soak up Southern California sunshine beside his swimming-pool. He was still working on the Douglas Fairbanks tan he'd been impressed with so many years before.

From the experience of poverty as a child, Grant was anything but extravagant. He had also made good investments with his savings. They brought in enough money to keep him quite free from worry. Additionally and maybe more importantly, his agent, Frank Vincent, had been busy. He had negotiated a commitment with Harry Cohn at Columbia Pictures for Cary Grant to make four movies for Columbia over two years (1937 and 1938). Grant was to be paid $50,000 each for the first two pictures and $75,000 each for the second pair. In 1937, Cary Grant had a quarter of a million dollar deal. He was 33 years old. Just five years previously, he had been signed for $450 a week, or less than $25,000 a year.

Grant was not alone as he sat by his pool at the beginning of the year. Many other movie folk gathered round. Howard Hughes and his new girlfriend, Ginger Rogers, were regulars. Marion Davies lived nearby and dropped in often. Grant's next-door neighbour came frequently, too. This was Hal Roach, a producer, director and screenwriter of comedies. He had worked with Harold Lloyd and was generally believed to be responsible for that famous comic's success. His other big successes included Laurel and Hardy and Our Gang.

Roach had a new project and he and Grant discussed it around the pool. The movie was *Topper*, an adaptation of the novel by Thorne Smith. It was the story of a fun-loving couple named George and Marion Kerby. Killed in a car accident, they can't get into heaven until they do a good deed on earth. They choose to spark up the life of a middle-aged man, a stuffy banker named Cosmo P. Topper.

Roach and Grant had great fun thinking of people to play the roles. They were both in love with the story. Grant thought Roach should cast Jean Harlow as Mrs Kerby and W. C. Fields as Topper. Roach knew who he wanted for Mr Kerby: Cary Grant. Grant told Roach he couldn't afford him. He was due to make $50,000 for the first Columbia picture. Roach kept bothering him to accept.

Finally, Grant agreed. The Columbia project wasn't due to begin until June and it looked as if *Topper* could be finished by then. He agreed to work for less money for Roach. Roach in turn agreed to make up the difference to $50,000 if the movie earned enough money. The other roles were filled by Constance Bennett as Marion Kerby, Roland Young as Topper and Billie Burke and Hedda Hopper played supporting parts. (Perhaps someone couldn't resist putting Hopper in *Topper*?)

Filming took place at Roach's little studio in Culver City, California. Norman Z. McCleod directed. His experience as an animator was important since *Topper*'s special effects provided many of the comic high points. Mr and Mrs Kerby had to appear and disappear, like any good ghosts. Animation and trick photography made it possible.

From time to time in the past, Cary Grant had been called a difficult person to work with. Unhappily, the *Topper* shoot was another one of those occasions. He, Roach and McCleod argued frequently about how the role of George Kerby should be played. Grant was a perfectionist, while Roach tended to let things happen. On top of that, Grant was not a fan of Constance Bennett and Bennett got top billing for the picture. He is said to have been relieved when filming was over.

Topper was released in July, 1937. It was a huge success, both critically and financially. What had been an irksome, annoying experience in the making turned out to be one of Cary Grant's most successful and important films.

Straight off the Paramount lot and the multitude of 'types' he'd been required to play, he was still developing the 'Cary Grant' screen persona. The charm and style of Mr Kerby proved to be immensely popular with the audience, making him more new fans. Never the fool, Grant took some of the aspects of that role for his permanent screen personality.

Immediately after work on *Topper* was finished, Grant went over to Columbia to make the first of his four-picture commitment to them. The film was called *The Awful Truth*.

Grant and his co-stars, Irene Dunne and Ralph Bellamy, were attracted to the project by its story: Lucy Warriner (Dunne) files for divorce from her suave, urbane husband,

Jerry (Grant). The action takes place during the 90-day waiting period before the divorce is made final. It concerns Jerry's reaction when he discovers that his soon-to-be-ex-wife is dating and intends to marry hayseed Oklahoma oil man, Daniel Leeson (Bellamy). Grant finds all this out when he returns to his old house to visit the family dog, played by Asta, the terrier in *The Thin Man*, and the most famous canine in America in those days. Dunne, in turn, tries to foil Grant's remarriage to aristocratic Molly Lamont.

This was a daring movie in 1937. To use divorce as a subject for comedy was just about unheard of. All three stars were drawn to the opportunity of doing something new. The film was directed by Leo McCarey.

Leo McCarey began his professional career as a lawyer, but quickly moved to the silver screen. He worked with Hal Roach as a gag writer and an executive at Roach's studios. He was recognized for having a real flair for comedy. He brought Laurel and Hardy together for the first time. He worked with Eddie Cantor, Mae West, W. C. Fields, and with the Marx Brothers in one of film comedy's brightest moments: *Duck Soup*. A few years after *The Awful Truth*, he made two Bing Crosby classics, *Going My Way*, for which he won two Academy Awards, and *The Bells of St Mary's*.

In the mid-1930s, he had left slapstick for light comedy, competing with the master of that style, Frank Capra. A dispute between Capra and Cohn led to McCarey being hired for *The Awful Truth*. Cohn wanted to do a 'Capra' movie without Capra.

McCarey's ability to blend humour and sentimentality earned him a reputation for brilliance. He was also known for being difficult and eccentric, although Jean Renoir, the famous French director, said of him, 'Leo McCarey is one of the few directors in Hollywood who understands human beings.' At the time, it's unlikely that Cary Grant would have agreed with Renoir's assessment. In later years, he came to appreciate him more.

Fresh from *Topper*, Grant brought his bad mood with him to *The Awful Truth*. He had problems with both his fellow actors and with McCarey.

In retrospect, Irene Dunne described the situation on the set. 'Cary used to be apprehensive about nearly everything in those days. So apprehensive, in fact, that he would almost get physically sick. If an actor, director or a scene displeased him, he would be greatly upset.' In truth, conditions on the set might have tried the patience of a saint. If *Topper* was a seat-of-the-pants production, *The Awful Truth* was more so.

When filming started, the actors were told they might not exactly follow the script they had been given. This was a classic understatement. McCarey showed up on the set each morning with script changes written on the back of paper bags. During the day, he and the screenwriter, Vina Delmar, improvised the staging.

What the actors didn't know was that the day before shooting started, McCarey had completely scrapped the existing script. He and Delmar were writing the next day's dialogue each night and then making up the staging to go along with the newly rewritten dialogue. Cary Grant was not happy. He found the whole atmosphere very upsetting. He argued with McCarey that he couldn't work under those conditions.

Harry Cohn headed Columbia production at the time. He was well known as a ruthless, vulgar man, despotic and outspoken. Perhaps the most hated and feared production chief of the day, he also had a sure instinct for what made a movie successful. Cary Grant was so unhappy and displeased with the filming of *The Awful Truth* that he went to Cohn and offered him $5,000 to let him out of the picture. Rumour has it that when McCarey heard of this he offered to donate $5,000 of his own if Cohn would agree. Grant went so far as to offer Columbia a free film if they'd replace him in this one.

Cohn, perhaps with his famous nose for success, did not agree. He still wanted to show Frank Capra up, and he believed McCarey could do it. Years later, Cohn described Cary Grant on that set as having been 'nervous, uncertain and insecure'. Filming rocked on to completion.

As so often happens, all the worrying was for nothing, all the angst forgotten or overwhelmed by the simple, golden fact: *The Awful Truth* was a huge success. The finished film was nothing

Archie Leach, the future Cary Grant, at the age of six. *Express Newspapers*

(*Left*) In pursuit of fame: a young and dashing Cary Grant. *Culver Pictures Inc.*

(*Facing page*) With his second wife, Barbara Hutton, heiress to the Woolworth fortune, in 1942. *Culver Pictures Inc.*

(*Below*) With Virginia Cherrill at a screening of *Supernatural* given by Paramount in 1933. They married in London in 1934. *Culver Pictures Inc.*

(*Above*) With Mae West in *She Done Him Wrong* (1933). *Movie Star News*

(*Below*) With Betsy Drake in *Every Girl Should Be Married* (1948). A year later they were. *Culver Pictures Inc.*

'So I turned to an actor, Walter Catlett, who had been a comic in the Ziegfeld Follies and I said, "Walter, have you been watching Miss Hepburn?" He said, "Yeah." "Will you tell her what she is doing wrong?" "Nope," he said. "Will you tell her if she asks?" I asked. "I guess I would have to," was his reply. So I went over to Kate and I said, "This isn't working but there is a man over there who I think can help. Will you go over and talk to him?" They talked and she came back and from that time on she knew how to play comedy better which is to just read the lines.'

Hawks was particularly grateful to Grant. He would always say Grant was probably his all-time favourite actor to work with. They went on to make three more films together. Hawks actually worked with Grant more than any other actor in his long career.

Incomprehensibly, *Baby* was not a commercial success. It had been a very expensive film to make, costing more than $1.2 million, a huge sum for the time. Cary Grant got $120,000 for his part. The movie lost more than $350,000 and further plunged the troubled studio into deep financial straits. Howard Hughes had to come along and bail out RKO by buying it.

Meanwhile at Columbia, money continued to roll in from *The Awful Truth*. The studio wanted to strike while the iron was still hot and team up Grant and Irene Dunne again. Their idea was to remake a big Broadway hit of the late 1920s called *Holiday*.

Adapted from the Philip Barry play, *Holiday* was to be a remake of a 1930 version which had been one of the first talkies. The inestimable Everett Edward Horton, perhaps the all-time master of the double-take, actually played the same supporting role in both movies. *Holiday* is the story of a non-conformist named Johnny Case involved with the daughter of a stuffy New York society family. He runs up against the girl's sister, who turns out to be a match for him. He falls in love with her.

Columbia signed on George Cukor to direct the picture and Cary Grant to play Johnny Case. Columbia wanted Irene Dunne to play the second sister. Cukor had a better idea.

Hepburn had understudied the role in the original Broadway show. Cukor liked the screen chemistry between Grant and Hepburn more than what happened between Grant and Dunne, even if the ticket-buying public did not necessarily agree. The script required frequent changes of mood and timing between the two characters. He insisted that Hepburn be given the role. To his enduring credit, Columbia chief Harry Cohn had the nerve to agree, even in the face of Hepburn's title of 'box-office poison'.

It was another outstanding performance by Cary Grant. Under Cukor's direction, he underplayed the role and even threw in some acrobatic tricks from his days with the Penders.

When this delightful comedy opened, it had a similar reception to that extended to *Bringing Up Baby* – great reviews, but a very lukewarm response from the box office. The movie ended up just about breaking even.

Holiday was a good personal showing for Cary Grant. *Newsweek* said, 'Cary Grant again turns in a smooth performance of the type that has made him one of Hollywood's most sought-after leading men.'

Each successive performance was bringing out more of him as an actor. He was feeling more comfortable and was becoming more willing to play different roles. What's more, his screen personality was becoming more defined. He believed he knew what roles he should be playing and he quickly made his requirements known.

Cary Grant realized that Hollywood's Dream Machine was not in the business of impressing movie critics, but of selling tickets. His value to producers was his ability to fill cinemas. His next picture needed to make money. If he had three losers in a row, he could end up in deep trouble – just as Hepburn now found herself.

For nearly a year, producer Pandro S. Berman had been getting a film ready for RKO loosely based on Rudyard Kipling's poem, 'Gunga Din'. Several years earlier, Berman had tried to make the movie with Ronald Colman and Spencer Tracy in two of the three almost equal male leads, but the project never got off the ground. Later, it was revived with Howard Hawks as director, but had to be put off again when Hawks started *Bringing Up Baby*. Now Berman was set to try to film the picture again, but he replaced Hawks with director George Stevens because RKO was not pleased with Hawks for having spent too much money making *Baby*.

Looking at this spectacular with its then-huge $2 million budget, Grant thought *Gunga Din* would be a sure winner. He spoke to Berman who cast him in the lead role of Ballantine, a soldier determined to leave the army for love. Douglas Fairbanks Jr was signed to play the second lead of Ballantine's friend, Cutter, and Victor McLaglen ('the Beloved Brute') signed on as the third male lead. The cast also included Joan Fontaine and Sam Jaffe.

The action took place in nineteenth-century India with the British soldiers fighting Indian punjabs. Waterboy Sam Jaffe saves the day in this British Empire epic. Shooting had already begun when Cary Grant's vision of his screen persona crystallized. He realized what he was doing was wrong. He felt he was much better suited for the role of Cutter and went to Berman to ask if he and Fairbanks could switch roles. Both Berman and director Stevens were startled to see an actor give up the lead for a second lead, but Stevens realized he would get a better performance from Grant if he was in a role in which he was more comfortable. The switch was made. Berman even agreed, at Grant's request, to change Cutter's first name to Archibald, a sort of inside joke.

As the filming went on, it became clear that Grant had been right. He was much better in the role of Cutter. Cutter had an undercurrent of humour in his character, a trait missing in Ballantine, who was more of a straight swashbuckler.

George Stevens, who would later win Best Director Academy Awards for *A Place in the Sun* and for *Giant*, directed *Gunga Din*'s cast to uniformly excellent performances. He allowed Grant to improvise physical action and occasionally ad lib lines.

A recent digest of movies still calls *Gunga Din* 'THE Hollywood action-adventure yarn'. Released in 1939, it was the year's second highest grossing movie, surpassed only by

Henry Fonda's *Jesse James*. The studio's most expensive picture of the decade to make – 600 cast and crew on location for 75 days – it was nonetheless RKO's most profitable movie in years.

Cary Grant ended up with the box-office hit he had wanted. More than that, he simply loved the finished product. In later years, he would call it one of his two or three favourite films.

Next, Grant had been prepared to start a movie with Ginger Rogers, to be directed by Leo McCarey. Unfortunately both Rogers and McCarey became ill and *Once Upon a Honeymoon* was postponed for some time.

Grant immediately went to work on another Howard Hawks aviator-adventure film, *Only Angels Have Wings*. A good story, the picture was about a group of pilots who run a mail service across the Andes in South America. It was filled with spectacular aerial scenes and plane crashes.

This was a very personal film for Hawks. It featured the kind of men he liked and spent time with. He said, 'I knew every character in that picture. I knew how they thought and how they talked. Some critics said I went too far in the film but there wasn't a single scene in the whole film that wasn't real.'

It also turned out to be a somewhat difficult film for Hawks to make. As he remembers, 'Cary, of course, was great. He took to the role instantly. But I had real trouble with the women.'

The film's female lead was Jean Arthur as a showgirl in love with Grant. For whatever reason, Hawks just couldn't reach her. 'She didn't fit into the type of girl that I liked,' he would comment later. 'She'd simply say, "I can't do that type of stuff." She was afraid to do anything on the spur of the moment. I think she is the only person that I ever worked with that I didn't help a bit.'

The second female lead was even more difficult. Harry Cohn's latest find was a stunningly beautiful young actress named Rita Hayworth. Hawks had developed a reputation of being very helpful to new actresses, so Cohn cast her in the second lead as a woman bored with her husband. Cohn told Hawks to 'make her a star'. Unfortunately, she was extremely self-conscious, not at all spontaneous, and at this point in her young career, not a particularly good actress.

Hawks turned to Cary Grant for help. He had a wicked gift
for working with young actresses. At his urging, several scenes
were restaged. In one scene, Hayworth was supposed to cry
but it wasn't happening. A lunch break was called and Hawks
and Grant conferred. When shooting resumed, the scene was
moved outdoors and a rain machine was brought in. Hayworth
was so soaking wet, you couldn't tell if it was tears or rain on
her face.

In another scene, Hawks couldn't get the right reaction from
Hayworth. He held another conference with Grant, and they
decided that Grant should suddenly pour a jug of iced water
over Hayworth's head. They didn't tell her what they were
going to do. They got the reaction the scene needed. On
another occasion, Hayworth was supposed to be drunk. She
could not get her lines right. Finally, Grant suggested that she
simply sag down and he would in effect do his lines and hers,
too. It worked. Critics later gave her kudos for playing a great
drunk scene.

The film emerged successful. *Newsweek* commented, 'Grant
is perfectly cast in the leading role.' It made a lot of money for
Columbia and Cohn was particularly happy with the job
Hawks had done with Hayworth. Hawks recalled, 'He gave me
a new car and said I had given him a star.'

Now Cary Grant listened to his instincts again. He had just
completed two action-adventure films in which women
appeared only coincidentally. He had an offer from Columbia
to do another adventure and an offer from RKO to do a screwball comedy, but he felt what he needed now was a love story.

He found it in what was considered a 'small' film, *In Name
Only*, a pet project of Pandro Berman. This was a high-class
soap opera about a rich man unhappily married to a socialite.
He falls in love with a sweet young widow. His wife, however,
refuses to divorce him and at the movie's end, the audience is
left up in the air about whether he and the widow will live happily ever after together or not.

In Name Only starred Kay Francis as the gold-digger wife and
Carole Lombard as the young widow. It was probably before its
time. To the movie-going public, Cary Grant meant either

comedy or adventure, but this was dark melodrama. It was not terribly successful. However, Grant gave a moving performance and showed that he was becoming a better and better actor. He really deserved more recognition for the effort. More than one critic has picked *In Name Only* as his most underrated film.

If *In Name Only* was a disappointment to him, his next project certainly raised his spirits. For almost a year, director Howard Hawks had wanted to remake *Front Page*, the Ben Hecht story that had been a major Broadway hit in the 1920s. Howard Hughes had already made it into a film in 1931.

Front Page is the story of an ace newspaper reporter, Hildy Johnson, who decides to leave the paper, and Walter Burns, a conniving editor, who does not want to let the reporter go. Hawks had bought the rights from Hughes, but wished to make a critical change in the story.

In both the original play and Hughes' 1931 film version, the reporter was a man. Hawks wanted to make Hildy a woman and have romance enter the plot, something that was missing from the play and the original film. Hawks remembers that the idea came to him one night at dinner. 'I called (author Ben) Hecht in New York and I said, "What do you think of making Hildy into a woman?" He said, "I wish I had thought of that." Then he said he would come out and help me and he did.'

When the new script was finished, Hawks went to talk to Harry Cohn. Cohn liked the idea of remaking *Front Page* and suggested Walter Winchell as the editor and Cary Grant as the reporter. Hawks explained that he wanted Hildy to be a woman and introduce a love interest. Cohn was doubtful. After all, *Front Page* had become something of a national institution. But he had a lot of faith in Hawks and in the Hawks-Grant combination. So Cohn said he would produce the film if Grant would play the editor. Grant quickly agreed. The movie was retitled *His Girl Friday*.

Hawks had trouble finding an actress to play Johnson. Virtually a Who's Who of the leading actresses of the day turned him down. Someone suggested a relative newcomer to Hollywood, Rosalind Russell. Hawks tested her and liked her immediately. He thought she'd be great opposite Cary Grant. Hawks was right. Cary Grant and Rosalind Russell were just about perfect together.

In this movie, Hawks used what was a daring technique for the times. He not only allowed his two stars to improvise a lot of their lines, but encouraged them to speak over one another. Traditionally, in movie dialogue, first one character spoke and then the other. In this quick-fire give and take, one would start speaking well before the other finished.

Occasionally, Grant and Russell would be completely flabbergasted by some ad lib, like Grant's 'The last time anyone said that to me, it was Archie Leach the week before he cut his throat.' Another time, Russell, improvising, suddenly throws her handbag at Grant, but misses him. Without batting an eyelid, he sadly looks at her and sighs, 'You used to have better aim than that.' Even the very last line of the film was ad libbed. Grant and Russell are going off together to live happily ever after. Russell is carrying the bags. Looking at her, Grant shakes his head sadly. 'Can't you do a better job of carrying than that?' he asks.

By now, Grant worked so well with Hawks that they had developed a shorthand. Hawks explained, 'I'd say to Cary, "This is a perfect chance to do number seven." Number seven was trying to talk to a woman who was doing a lot of talking. We'd just do number seven and he'd find variations on that. He was such a great receiver. He was so marvellous.'

A lot of people have written about Cary Grant and his leading ladies. Some argue that he worked best with Grace Kelly or Ingrid Bergman or Katharine Hepburn or Audrey Hepburn. But Hawks and many others believe his best screen match was Rosalind Russell in *His Girl Friday*. Unhappily, the two never worked together again, for no particular reason. They did stay lifelong friends. Russell even married Freddie Brisson, a London agent whom Grant had introduced to her. In fact, he was best man at their wedding.

The critics loved *His Girl Friday*, and it went on to become another commercial success for Cary Grant.

Grant made one more movie in 1940. Ever since the success

of *The Awful Truth*, Leo McCarey had been trying to find another film to team up Grant with Irene Dunne once again. Now he had the project: *My Favourite Wife*.

A sequel to *The Awful Truth*, the plot has Irene Dunne, supposedly long dead in a plane crash, coming back to the US to find her husband, Grant, has remarried. She has lived the past seven years on a desert island with a slightly daft scientist played by Randolph Scott.

McCarey was going to direct the picture, but just before filming started he was in a serious car accident. RKO brought in the young director Garson Kanin, then 29, who had just finished doing a Ginger Rogers movie. When McCarey could leave hospital, he rushed back to the set. Reportedly, he wasn't happy with some of Kanin's work and reshot some scenes and shot several new ones. Despite having two directors, the film turned out to be witty, fun and just plain good. It was part slapstick, part sly comedy.

The critics liked it, with *The New York Times* commenting, 'Another delightful picture with Cary Grant and Irene Dunne chasing each other around most charmingly in it.' Audiences loved it, too. *My Favourite Wife* made over $750,000 for RKO. Cary Grant was now its top box-office draw.

He felt it was time to change gears again. He had just done two comedies, so for his next project he let Harry Cohn at Columbia talk him into a real change of pace. *The Howards of Virginia* takes place during the Revolutionary War. The story, based on a best-selling novel, is about a backwoodsman who marries an aristocrat. Cohn convinced Grant it would broaden his appeal and he brought Frank Lloyd in to direct. Lloyd had directed *Mutiny on the Bounty* and had a reputation for being the best period piece director in Hollywood.

Not even Lloyd's considerable talents could save this one. It wasn't a bad movie, but Cary Grant in buckskin and ponytail was just plain silly. He was obviously uncomfortable and he showed it almost every minute he was on the screen. *The Howards* was a disaster at the box office and ended Grant's string of hits. It also convinced him that he should never again play a character role and never again be caught dead in a

CARY GRANT: MOVIE STAR

costume period piece. *Newsweek* said, 'Obviously miscast, Cary Grant meets the exigencies of a difficult role with more gusto than persuasion.'

The opportunity to get back into a real 'Cary Grant' role presented itself with *The Philadelphia Story*. The project had been created for Katharine Hepburn. She was given the right to choose her director and her leading men. She chose George Cukor to direct and then called Grant. He was offered top billing and $150,000 plus percentages. He jumped at the chance to co-star with Hepburn and Jimmy Stewart, the second male lead. It turned out to be a good choice.

Filming began in July, 1940. Cukor ran a very loose set. He let his actors develop their own characters and ad lib lines to fit those characters. Grant played the role of C. K. Dexter Haven, ex-husband of society girl Tracy Lord (Hepburn). She is on the eve of her second marriage. Stewart played the reporter sent to cover the event.

Grant played his role as a witty, romantic, debonair, but somewhat elusive man of the world, all very understated. It was a perfect foil to Hepburn's strength. There was a bite to this romantic comedy that still keeps it superior to its 1956 remake – *High Society* with Bing Crosby, Grace Kelly and Frank Sinatra – as good as that later film was.

The Philadelphia Story opened the first week of 1941 to rave reviews. Critics liked the movie and each of the stars. One said, 'Grant is perfectly gracious in a thankless part, winning sympathy and belief.'

It played New York's Radio City Music Hall for over six weeks, breaking all the house box-office records. The only other movie that made more money that year was Gary Cooper's *Sergeant York*. The film also more or less rescued Kate Hepburn's career. It proved, once and for all, that she could make a film that would succeed with the public.

As good as the reviews were, as exciting as the audience approval was, and as rewarding as the earnings were, *The Philadelphia Story* intensified one of the big disappointments of Grant's life. He was about the only person on the picture not to be nominated for an Academy Award.

When Jimmy Stewart earned Best Actor, Grant remembered that he had been able to choose which role he played in the movie. He still believed, quite correctly, that he had chosen well. Nonetheless, he felt he was unappreciated by the Hollywood community and admitted to sharp disappointment. That feeling continued to grow over the years.

By the beginning of 1941, Cary Grant was unarguably and certifiably a major Movie Star. His name alone on a movie marquee guaranteed activity at the box office. He could name his own salary. But the memory of the poverty of young Archie Leach never left him. He remained frugal. He and Randy Scott continued to share the house in Santa Monica. He'd always loved cars, and he gave in to the Tinseltown trend to drive expensive, flashy automobiles. On an uncharacteristic spending spree he bought himself a Cord convertible. He sold it within a few weeks, though, realizing ostentation was not his style.

Grant was not a frequent guest at the big Hollywood parties. He preferred to entertain at home. When he did go out, it was often to David Chasen's new little restaurant. He and many others felt comfortable there because Chasen refused to let in autograph-hounds.

Grant was not pleased by autograph-seekers. In an interview with Louella Parsons, he once said, 'This autograph evil, and I do consider it an evil, has gotten entirely out of hand. Originally it was charming, every player is grateful for admiration. To scrawl your name on a piece of paper does not seem the thing, but to be torn apart and insulted while you're writing it, several hundred times wherever you go, then it becomes intolerable.' Grant always protected his privacy, even at the height of his stardom.

When Cary Grant, Rosalind Russell and Howard Hawks made *His Girl Friday* in 1940, they took the screwball comedy of the 1930s to its limits. It seemed clear to everyone, including Grant, that this particular type of movie had reached its end. Grant knew he had done as much as he could with it, and decided to move on.

The role of 'Cary Grant' was beginning to be something the

man played well. He had found what he felt was his perfect niche: light comedy. Just at this point, his career took a surprise shift. The contract he had made with Columbia in 1937 still had one more movie on it. The contract had been extended several times. Harry Cohn insisted in his well-known obnoxious manner that Grant do a picture called *Penny Serenade* opposite, again, Irene Dunne. Grant did not want to do it. He was convinced he should play light comedy and this was a heavy melodrama. Cohn had been wrong about *The Howards* and Grant thought he was wrong this time.

Once again, he went to Harry Cohn and tried to buy himself out of the picture. Once again, Harry Cohn refused. Irene Dunne later remembered, 'Cary thought it was all too serious.' Cary Grant did find two silver linings in the cloud. For one thing, the shooting schedule was short. For another, he was paid $100,000.

George Stevens directed *Penny Serenade*, described by a modern critic as 'a wonderful tearjerker'. Dunne and Grant play a couple whose marriage is on the rocks after they lose a baby. They try to pull things back together by adopting a child.

As with *The Awful Truth*, Harry Cohn was right about *Penny Serenade*. The critics gave it good reviews, and Grant finally received an Academy Award nomination. One review said, 'Cary Grant is thoroughly good, in some ways to the point of surprise, for there is not only that easy swing and hint of the devil in him, but faith and passion expressed, the character held together where it might so easily have fallen into the component parts of too good, too silly, etc.' Another commented, 'Grant turns in a surprising performance as he fills the dramatic requirements of this serious role.'

Although he did not win the Best Actor Oscar, the nomination and the good reviews made him less wary of filming dramas. He felt more confident about playing a wider variety of characters.

For a man who had decided to do only light comedy just one movie ago, Grant's next picture proved to be an even greater departure from this goal.

During the *Penny Serenade* shoot, Grant had agreed to follow that film with one for RKO. For the new project, RKO recruited an Englishman as director. The man had won an outstanding reputation for himself in England between 1934 and 1939 making a series of superb suspense dramas which included *The Man Who Knew Too Much* and *The Thirty-Nine Steps*. Both were huge commercial and critical successes around the world. He was, of course, the incomparable Alfred Hitchcock, movie-dom's all-time master of suspense.

After David O. Selznick wooed him for two years, Hitchcock finally came to America in 1940. Had it not been for the out-break of World War II, he might not have done so. But with war clouds gathering in 1939, the British film industry was going to go out of movie-making and into the propaganda business, so Hitchcock agreed to come to Hollywood.

His first project for Selznick was an adaptation of Daphne du Maurier's *Rebecca*. Hitchcock took this gothic romance and successfully turned it into a psychological suspense drama. Its superb direction helped *Rebecca* to win the Oscar for Best Picture of 1940 and to get Hitchcock a Best Director nomination. Selznick immediately offered Hitchcock a three-year contract. The director set about looking for projects and one of the first he found was one then called *Before The Fact*.

RKO had been trying to get this movie off the ground since 1935 when they had bought the rights to a British novel of the same name. The book was a chilling story of a plain-looking wealthy woman, newly married and so desperately in love with her young, handsome husband that she overlooks the fact that he is a philanderer, a criminal and finally a murderer. When she realizes that he is about to kill her for her money, she finds out at the same time that she is pregnant. Desperate to keep him, as the wife in the film says, 'from reproducing himself', she writes and seals a suicide note telling the authori-ties everything, gives it to her husband to post and calmly drinks a glass of poisoned milk he has given her.

In 1935, RKO wanted Emlyn Williams to play the husband, but the project never came to anything. In 1939, Robert Mont-gomery was approached for the role but that was put aside temporarily when Laurence Olivier said that he wanted to do the part. While the studio debated over whether to let Olivier play a murderer, Alfred Hitchcock came on the scene.

Hitchcock always maintained that he felt the film should be true to the book with the wife no longer wanting to live, writing the letter indicting the husband, and the husband posting his own incrimination as the ending.

The studio still could not see Olivier as a cold-blooded murderer, but he remained the leading candidate for the role. So, according to film historians, Hitchcock was given the project when he convinced studio executives that he could change the story to be about a woman's paranoia. She would *think* her husband was trying to kill her, but whether he was or wasn't would be left to the audience to decide.

Hitchcock wanted Joan Fontaine, who had starred for him in *Rebecca*, to play the wife. He saw the film as an elegant psychological thriller and decided he wanted Cary Grant to play the murdering cad. Hitchcock and Grant knew each other socially since both were leading members of the growing British colony in Hollywood. Grant, with his new confidence for drama from his role in *Penny Serenade*, was willing to give it a try.

Even when filming began, no one had yet decided how it would end. Hitchcock started to talk about reverting to the straightforward ending of the book. However, neither Grant nor RKO could see Grant as a callous murderer, any more than Olivier. They argued for the revised ending, with the crime in the mind of the neurotic woman. The writing and rewriting of possible endings continued during shooting.

The controversy carried over into the simple question of naming the film. At first, Hitchcock wanted to call it *Fright* and the studio wanted *Suspicious Lady*. At one point, RKO hired the Gallup polling organization to test more than 50 titles in on-the-street interviews all over the country. Among the titles tested were *Men Make Poor Husbands*, *Love in Irons* and *Last Lover*. Reportedly, the top-rated title was *Search for Tomorrow* but everyone agreed that made no sense, so the Gallup results were junked.*

* Years later when a television producer was looking for a name for his new soap opera, he remembered this same story and called his daytime drama *Search for Tomorrow*. It has run successfully for years.

Filming of what Hollywood was now calling 'Hitchcock's no-name film' began on February 10. By July, there was still no ending. Hitchcock still wanted to end it with the murder; then the studio put another obstacle in his way. They said they thought the Hays Office censors would never approve of a pregnant woman committing suicide. There were more than a dozen possible endings, at least on paper, including one where it turns out the baby is not her husband's and that's why the wife agrees to let herself be poisoned.

To say all this had a poor effect on the cast would be an understatement. They were confused, especially Fontaine. How could she act if she didn't know whether she was facing a murderer or whether she was crazy and her husband was just a gold-digger? Her performance in *Rebecca* had been good because of Hitchcock's firm direction. But here, he couldn't be much help since he himself didn't know which ending the studio would approve.

Amazingly, while all this was going on, Cary Grant became a kind of rock of stability on the shaky set. Something strange happened during this film. Cary Grant frequently distrusted directors and constantly worried about the most minor incidents that took place on a set.

With Hitchcock, Grant was a changed man. He trusted him completely. Although their public images were miles apart, in fact they were very similar. Both were aloof, cautious, and somewhat suspicious.

Cary Grant continued to be wary of directors for the rest of his career – with Hitchcock the notable exception. When he acted for Hitchcock, he let that genius mould him as he wished. Neither man was ever disappointed with the result of their work together over the next 20 years.

With this picture, the result was amazing. Hitchcock took Grant's usual sunny, handsome charm and turned it into something malevolent within the setting. This was even intensified by the ending that the studio finally dictated – the woman's fears are shown to be groundless – because all during the film the audience is never sure if it's actually watching a murder or is only seeing harmless actions made sinister through the wife's increasingly paranoid vision. (This ending was finally chosen after previewing several alternatives and measuring audience response.)

When filming was completed in August, the picture still didn't have a name. Only days before it was released in November, RKO decided on *Suspicion*, which was what Hitchcock himself had been calling it since early June. He had decided the film had to have some kind of name to allow the actors, especially Fontaine, some kind of focus.

When *Suspicion* opened, the critics couldn't say enough about how good it was. The *New York Times* wrote, 'Cary Grant finds a new field for himself, the field of crime, the smiling villain without heart or conscience.' *Variety* said, 'Grant puts conviction into his unsympathetic but arresting role.'

Modern reviewers have not been quite so kind to this movie. In Leonard Maltin's digest of movies, the entry for *Suspicion* says it leaves the viewer flat with its ending. Ephraim Katz, in his definitive *Film Encyclopedia*, writes that the movie was 'well-acted', that Grant gave the 'first of several solid appearances in Hitchcock films', but that 'Grant's presence weakened the plot in the end.'

Suspicion was nominated for Best Picture and Hitchcock for Best Director. Fontaine won the Best Actress Oscar. Grant was not mentioned.

If not perfect, *Suspicion* was nonetheless very good. It was RKO's biggest commercial success of 1941.

With *The Philadelphia Story*, *Penny Serenade* and *Suspicion*, Grant had appeared in three of 1941's highest grossing films. He was an unquestionable box-office draw, on a par with Clark Gable, Gary Cooper and Mickey Rooney. He was forever a Movie Star.

In 1941, people around the world were worried about a great deal more than a Hitchcock villain. There was a real villain in Germany. World War II was being fought in Europe, with Great Britain in the thick of it.

Grant was still British and greatly disturbed by the war clouds over Europe. The British press was attacking him for staying in Hollywood while his countrymen were at war. He

agonized over what to do. He had David Niven's sad example
before him. Immediately after war was declared, Niven had
first tried joining the Canadian Army and when turned down,
had made his way back to England and tried to enlist in the
RAF. He was turned down again and labelled a publicity
seeker.

Grant was extremely distressed when he learned in January
1940 that several of the Leaches, including his aunt, uncle,
their son and his wife, had been killed in an air raid on Bristol.

He and Sir Cedric Hardwicke, the unofficial head of the
British colony in Hollywood, went to Washington to meet
Lord Lothian, the British ambassador, to ask what they could
do to aid the British war effort. 'Carry on what you are doing,'
was the reply. So he returned to Hollywood where he donated
his entire $125,000 salary from *The Philadelphia Story* to the
war effort.

Nonetheless, Cary Grant knew himself to have become
more American than English after so many years in the United
States. California was his home. Soon after the Japanese
attacked Pearl Harbor and the US entered the war in
December, 1941, he legally changed his name to Cary Grant
and applied for American citizenship. It was granted the next
summer.

Also around the time of *The Philadelphia Story*, Cary Grant
fell in love again. Back in 1938, he had met the heiress to the
Woolworth fortune, Barbara Hutton, on an Atlantic crossing.
Now she stopped in California on her way to a holiday in Haw-
aii. While in Hollywood, the two met again. As with Virginia
Cherrill, it was love at first sight. Once again, the press took
immediately to this latest glamorous Hollywood romance.

In the meantime, Grant completed *The Philadelphia Story*,
Penny Serenade and *Suspicion*. He finished up 1941 with his
third movie of that year, *Arsenic and Old Lace*.

Arsenic and Old Lace is the story of a young man in Brooklyn
whose two elderly spinster aunts are poisoning old men who
come to the house. It was one of Broadway's longest-running
hits. Director Frank Capra bought the film rights and planned
to shoot it for Warner Brothers. Allyn Joslyn, who played the

role of the nephew, Mortimer Brewster, on Broadway would not be in the film. Capra wanted Bob Hope. He was unavailable. Capra and Jack Warner then called Frank Vincent to see if Cary Grant might be interested. The answer was 'maybe', on the condition that Warners, in addition to a $50,000 fee for Grant, would make a sizeable donation to British war relief.

As the negotiations dragged on, Grant flew to New York to see the play. Mortimer, on stage, was a supporting character to the two spinster aunts. He decided he'd only be interested in making the film if the role were significantly beefed up. Capra agreed to enlarge the part for Grant, and Jack Warner agreed to the war relief donation. Filming on *Arsenic and Old Lace* began in late October. The cast included Peter Lorre and Raymond Massey, who turned in excellent performances as two less than discerning murderers who hole up in the old ladies' home.

The movie was shot very quickly since the Broadway cast was available for only four weeks. What's more, Capra decided to shoot each scene in sequence, just as they'd be seen, an unusual technique in movies. Grant clearly did not respond to Capra as well as he had to Hitchcock. Consequently, he acted rather stiltedly, and the result can probably be best described as an uneven performance.

Grant himself came to hate the movie and to consider his performance in it the single worst of his career. Years later, he would say: 'I told Frank Capra. I said, "Frank, I simply cannot do this kind of comedy." And Frank said, "Of course you can, old boy." And I went ahead and did it and I overplayed it terribly. Terribly. Jimmy Stewart could have done a much better job than I did. He would have been wonderful in the part. I told Frank Capra that at the time. He just wouldn't listen.'

But the public would not get a chance to judge for some time. Capra had agreed not to release the movie until after the Broadway show had closed. He had not expected that the show would run for another three years. Although shot in 1941, *Arsenic and Old Lace* was not released until 1944. By that time, Cary Grant was such a hot property that the movie did quite well despite generally unfavourable reviews.

Pearl Harbor occurred about a week before the end of filming on *Arsenic and Old Lace*. America was now at war, but it still wanted to be entertained. Almost without pausing, Grant went on to his next project.

After the success of *Penny Serenade*, Columbia believed that Grant and director George Stevens made a winning team. The studio was developing a comedy-drama about a falsely accused murderer, Leopold Dilg, who hides out in a house rented by a law professor. The professor is being considered for the position of a Supreme Court Justice and is spending the summer writing a book. His landlady, who is in love with him, meets Dilg. Convinced of his innocence, she agrees to hide him and eventually falls in love with him. In this literate picture, Grant, as the fugitive, tries to convince Ronald Colman, the jurist, that there's a human side to the law. Jean Arthur played the landlady.

The movie was called *The Talk of the Town*. Its odd blend of comedy and drama made it a difficult script. The conflict in the plot centres on the love triangle. Through most of the story, it seems Colman will get the girl. At the very end, she seems to choose Cary Grant, although the audience is never quite sure.

Actually, Stevens shot three different endings, one in which Colman gets the girl, one in which Grant gets the girl and the ambiguous one. Again, various preview audiences were shown different endings. From their reactions, Stevens decided on the one he used. All things considered, it is a credit to the cast and their director that *The Talk of the Town* turned out to be both a commercial and critical success. It earned seven Academy Award nominations, although it won no Oscars.

Immediately after the filming, Grant left Hollywood on a month-long United Service Organizations (USO) tour, entertaining at military bases around the country. On the tour, Grant fell back on his vaudeville talents and played straight man to Bert Lahr in some classic old sketches.

He returned to Hollywood in time for the 1942 Academy Award ceremonies. Cary Grant was to receive yet another professional disappointment. He had been nominated for his role in *Penny Serenade*. He lost. What's more, he lost to his old rival, Gary Cooper, who took the Oscar for *Sergeant York*.

Grant had always wanted to work with Ginger Rogers but he had never had the chance. Therefore, he was happy to accept an offer from Leo McCarey to star opposite her in the previously delayed *Once Upon a Honeymoon* for RKO. The movie was an adventure-comedy with Grant as an American correspondent in Europe who meets a former American burlesque queen, Rogers. She has just married a baron. The baron, played by Walter Slezak, is also secretly an evil Nazi agent. In the film, Grant unmasks the Nazi and in the process falls in love with Rogers, who unsurprisingly throws over the baron when his activities are revealed.

Filming on this picture was briefly held up a couple of times while Cary Grant took breaks for some very important personal business. The first event was citizenship. Grant officially became an American on June 26, 1942, at the age of 38.

In early July, he took a second short break. He and Barbara Hutton were married. Press-shy from his wedding to Virginia Cherrill, the ceremony took place in the back garden of Frank Vincent's vacation home at Lake Arrowhead. Just a few close friends were present. Ironically, the next day he was back at RKO continuing *Once Upon a Honeymoon*. He himself had no time for a honeymoon.

Although he had made a deal with Randy Scott that whoever remarried first would get their beloved house in Santa Monica, Grant moved out and sold his share to Scott. Barbara bought a large house from Douglas Fairbanks in Pacific Palisades. The couple, along with her six-year-old son, Lance, from her marriage to Count Haugwitz-Reventlow, moved into the new home.

After settling in, Grant decided to take some time off. Then the tennis pro at his club told him about an idea for a movie. In the great Hollywood tradition of those days, almost before you could blink, a script had been turned out and cameras were rolling at RKO on *Mr Lucky*.

Grant played the owner of a gambling ship who tries to fleece a female passenger. Instead, he falls in love and goes straight. The movie became the basis for a later television series.

In another of those strange twists of fate, *The Talk of the Town* and *Once Upon a Honeymoon*, both carefully crafted films, were box-office disappointments. The hastily thrown together *Mr Lucky* was a big hit. After its release in May, 1943, it became RKO's biggest profit-maker of the year.

After *Mr Lucky*, Grant decided he was due to have some time off. For the next few months he devoted himself to Barbara and Lance, leaving only for some tours of military bases for the USO.

The press, probably because of Barbara's great fortune, began to refer to the couple as 'Cash and Cary'. In the days before feminism, he was called 'Mr Barbara Hutton'. This was ironic since, privately and at his own request, he had signed a prenuptial agreement giving up any claim to Hutton's vast wealth.

In the summer of 1943, Jack Warner of Warner Brothers decided to produce a major war movie. What's more, he wanted it out in the cinemas before Christmas. With the more complicated technology of that day, this was not as easy as it had been ten years before.

Warner signed Cary Grant to play the lead in *Destination Tokyo*, the story of a US submarine in Japanese waters and the interaction among the crew. (Imagine Grant with an all-male cast!) Grant played the sub's commander.

Destination Tokyo went before the cameras in September. Because the shooting of this picture was done in a rush, the work was long and hard. Grant was on the set by dawn and didn't leave until after dark. He spent his nights learning his lines for the next day. Barbara didn't much care for this kind of schedule. She had grown used to having him around when she wanted him. She was angry and unhappy about sharing her husband with his work.

When *Destination Tokyo* opened, the reviewers raved. One said Grant 'gave one of the soundest performances of his career'. Ticket sales were brisk.

Cary Grant was professionally happy, but his marriage was

in trouble. He wanted to work, and things were going well for him, but Barbara wanted him home. It was becoming evident how little the two of them had in common.

The problem was made worse when Grant immediately started work on another film. He wanted a change of pace again and *Once Upon a Time* was about as lighthearted a comedy as you could imagine. It was the silly story of a down and out Broadway producer who gives his last dime to a young boy. The boy turns out to have a tap-dancing caterpillar named 'Curley the Wonder Worm'. The producer expertly guides Curley to become a major hit, the money rolls in, and the producer is saved. Unsurprisingly, when the movie opened in 1944, it did nowhere as well as the worm.

Understandably, Grant was a little embarrassed by *Once Upon a Time*. He began to look for a project with some dramatic substance. Early in 1944, RKO was developing a movie based on the novel *None but the Lonely Heart*. The screenplay was being written by playwright Clifford Odets. (Odets and Grant would become lifelong friends.)

RKO wanted Grant to play the lead, a Cockney drifter named Ernie Mott. Mott becomes a thief to support his dying mother, played by Ethel Barrymore. She in turn opens a second-hand shop to fence stolen goods so she'll have something to leave her son. Grant really wanted to do this straight drama. He felt it was time for him to play more serious roles, and this was to be a serious role indeed.

Odets was a little unsure when he first heard the studio wanted to cast Grant in the role. He had imagined Ernie Mott as much younger, probably a teenager. But the more he thought about it, the more he agreed with the studio. Grant would be perfect for the role. He rewrote parts of the script to make the character older and to tailor the dialogue to fit Grant. He was more than gratified when Grant insisted that the playwright be allowed to direct. The cast also included Barry Fitzgerald, Jane Wyatt, and Dan Duryea. Ethel Barrymore was to win the Oscar for Best Supporting Actress for her role in the picture.

Shortly before the filming finished in April, the Grant

household faced a crisis. Lance had been living with his father and stepmother in New York for the last six months and was due to return to California. Count Reventlow now refused to send him back to his mother. He filed suit to gain custody. Grant and Barbara countersued. Their anguish brought them back together. It soon became clear that in fact things had not changed between them. In August, they separated.

A month later, *None but the Lonely Heart* was released. The reviews were outstanding. The *Hollywood Reporter* stated Ernie Mott was 'the finest thing he (Grant) has ever done'. (Modern critics continue to like this movie, but point out that it suffered from the censorship of the times, as well as the World War II rhetoric.)

This was followed by the long-awaited release of *Arsenic and Old Lace*. The reviews were again terrific. One critic said, 'Grant scores remarkably well.' Another wrote, '(Grant) carries this picture with pantomime, facial expressions and a wild sort of farcical delivery of lines. He is a master of that.'

According to the old saying, 'When you're up, you're up'. Cary and Barbara became reconciled at this point. He determined to work to make his marriage succeed. He refused all the scripts that were offered to him. It was during this period that he turned down the opportunity to play the witty, sophisticated bon vivant, Cole Porter.

Jack Warner had acquired the rights to do a film biography of Cole Porter. Porter was a personal friend of Grant's and he wanted Grant to portray him in the film. Warner knew that Harry Cohn at Columbia was angry with Grant, so he asked Cohn to lend him Grant to make the film. When Cohn balked, Warner made him an almost unprecedented offer: Humphrey Bogart, Warner's number one box-office attraction, in exchange for Grant. Cohn knew that Grant was furious with Columbia for *Once Upon a Time* and that at least for the short term, his relationship with Grant was at a low point. So he sold Grant's contract, which had one film left on it, to Warner.

Warner tried everything he could think of to persuade Grant to do the Cole Porter film. It was to be directed by Michael Curtiz who had just won the Academy Award for *Casablanca*. But

Grant stayed firm. He insisted on trying to save his marriage. He would turn down all work to give Barbara whatever time she wanted. Sadly, the reconciliation didn't last long. In February, 1945, Barbara left. The two issued a brief statement, 'After much thought and with great consideration, we have decided we can be happier living apart.'

Just a week later, the Oscar nominations were released. Grant was included for *None but the Lonely Heart*. Popular wisdom said he would win. It wasn't to be. The award for Best Actor went to Bing Crosby for *Going My Way*.

Cary Grant now began what was to be a very low period in his life. He had two failed marriages and it seemed to him that Hollywood might never come to appreciate him.

7

RECOVERY

AFTER HIS SEPARATION FROM Barbara and what felt like a humiliating loss at the Oscars, Cary Grant needed to heal his soul.

All things considered, he knew it was better for Barbara and him to be apart; and this particular Oscar loss was not in itself the end of the world. But when he looked at his life, at his two failed marriages, the dark clouds loomed large. For all his success with women on screen, for all that millions of adoring female fans wanted him, his track record with the fair sex was not very good in real life.

And then, just to make matters worse, his industry ignored him. He worked very hard at his profession, he got better and better as an actor, his films earned huge profits for the industry, but his peers refused to honour him. No awards came his way, while all around him others were being acclaimed for lesser achievements than his own. Grant retreated into himself. For weeks he did nothing at all. His friends tried to bring him out of his depression. Nothing helped.

Finally, one day he gave himself a mental shake. It was time to go back to doing what he did best. It was time to work again.

Grant called up Jack Warner. Warner still wanted him to do the movie biography of Cole Porter. Cole Porter still wanted Cary Grant to play his life. Anyone who thought about it knew it was a natural. Cary Grant agreed to do the picture.

Production on *Night and Day* started in June, 1945. Almost

from the first day there was a raging battle between Grant and the movie's director, Mike Curtiz.

Curtiz was an interesting man. Born in Budapest in 1885, he began working in film there as early as 1912. After World War I, he took political refuge in Germany and Austria and proceeded to make movies throughout Europe. In 1926, Curtiz was brought to Hollywood by Harry Warner. Over the next 25 years, he made well over 100 pictures for Warner Brothers. He did excellent work with Errol Flynn, Humphrey Bogart and Jimmy Cagney. His *Mildred Pierce* in 1945 would establish Joan Crawford in movie history. His *Casablanca* in 1942 is one of the most enduring popular movies ever made. He earned Oscar nominations and won them. But Curtiz was not a nice man. Perhaps the complete opposite of George Cukor, the 'actor's director', Curtiz was purely and simply a dictator.

Studios still ran most actors' lives by holding long-term contracts on them. Curtiz, supposedly on the artistic side of moviemaking rather than the business end, almost always sided with his studio. Historians say Curtiz and Warner Brothers were one and the same.

With the exception of Harry Cohn at Columbia, Michael Curtiz was probably the most hated man in Hollywood. He ruled his movie sets with an iron hand, modelling himself on the fabled Cecil B. De Mille. Like Cohn, he was an enormous success. Just like the classic image of a movie director in old films, he wore jodhpurs and high boots and carried a riding crop under one arm.

He was known for his ability to make huge action scenes with casts of thousands. Not only was he a dictator, but he was also sadistic. He liked realism in his films. If this meant real blood, all the better. 'Nothing excited him more than real blood,' Errol Flynn remembered in his biography.

The list of stars who refused to work with Curtiz was a long one. Many of Warners' leading contract players insisted that their contracts include clauses saying they would never have to be directed by him.

Grant knew all the stories about Curtiz. But he took pride in being a professional. He knew that, whatever his personality,

Curtiz was more than talented. Grant felt that if someone had enough talent, he could manage to get along with him.

He was wrong.

On the set, Cary Grant and Michael Curtiz started clashing right from the beginning. It didn't help Grant's frame of mind that three weeks into the shoot, Barbara Hutton formally filed for divorce. By the end of the second month of filming the joke around Warner's was that the only way the war between Grant and Curtiz was going to end was if Truman dropped the atomic bomb on the set. If that's what it took to end the war with Japan, that's what it would take to make peace between Grant and Curtiz.

On the last day of filming *Night and Day* Grant is said to have delivered a speech that's a Hollywood legend. In a loud, solemn voice, in front of the entire cast and crew, Grant announced, 'If I'm ever a chump enough to work with you again, you'll know I'm either broke or I've lost my mind.' He never did work with Curtiz again. To his credit, as a professional, he did later send a telegram of appreciation to Curtiz after seeing the final cut of the movie.

The movie included a not-too-bad performance by Grant singing 'You're the Top'. The highlight of the film is probably Mary Martin's 'My Heart Belongs to Daddy'. It was a stellar cast. Besides Grant and Martin, it featured Alexis Smith, Jane Wyman, Eve Arden, Alan Hale and Dorothy Malone.

Night and Day was not the worst film ever made. It was better than *Sylvia Scarlett*, but it was far from a good movie. Its music was wonderful and this was what saved it, along with Grant's name. Most reviewers ended up calling it entertaining or something similar. Most people also said the plot was 'confused', which it was. But the public loved it.

The movie grossed $14 million at the box office, an astonishing sum in those days. It was the most money a Cary Grant movie had made to that date. What's more, the deal he had signed with Jack Warner gave him a percentage of the profits.

Within the industry, Grant was given credit for turning a poor film into a box-office hit. Studio executives started to ask themselves, 'If Grant can make that much money with a lousy picture, what can he do with something good?' All in all, *Night and Day* might not have been very much fun for Grant to make (and in later years he would point to it as one of his worst films), but it turned out to be very successful. It did an especially good job of enhancing his reputation.

Cary Grant wanted to keep working, but once again he had an identity problem. It was the same thing that had nagged at him before. Should he play drama or comedy? He'd proved in *Penny Serenade*, *Suspicion* and *None but the Lonely Heart* that he could play serious roles and play them well. Still, there was always that tug back to the light comedy that had made up so much of his early career. Here he was, a first-class movie star, but he still had a professional identity crisis. Which way should he go?

The question answered itself with his next two films. He came finally to realize that he could do both drama and comedy. That film personality we all know as 'Cary Grant' was about to crystallize, once and for all.

After all the nastiness on the set of *Night and Day*, his top priority for the next movie was to work with a director he could trust, one who ran a sane production. For Cary Grant, that spelled Alfred Hitchcock. Even while *Night and Day* was still being filmed, David O. Selznick asked him to work with Hitchcock. He wasted no time saying 'Yes!' After the hell of months working with Curtiz, he was thrilled to be back with a director who just told his actors what he wanted and then let them do it.

The picture was *Notorious*. It was Grant's second movie with Hitchcock. In its way, it turned out to be almost as important to his career as *Sylvia Scarlett* was.

His co-star on *Notorious* was Ingrid Bergman. She had just won the Academy Award for *Gaslight*. Bergman had come to Hollywood in 1939 from Sweden. She had become the most promising young actress on the Swedish screen while still in her teens. In 1936, she made a Swedish film called *Intermezzo*. She was just 21 years old.

Intermezzo was a sensation all over Europe. It's the story of a famous violinist, an older, married man, who falls in love with a young pianist, Bergman. It made its way to New York where one of Selznick's aides saw it and loved it. She persuaded Selznick to remake the picture in English. When she found that Bergman herself could speak English, she twisted Selznick's arm until he agreed to ask the young actress to come over and make the English version of the film.

The Hollywood *Intermezzo* was shot towards the end of 1939, with Leslie Howard as the violinist. By the time it was released, Bergman had gone back to Europe to make more movies there. When *Intermezzo* opened in the US, it was an even bigger hit than it had been in Europe. Bergman was an instant sensation. Unlike her countrywoman, Greta Garbo, who 'wanted to be alone', Bergman was natural, open, charming, and the ideal of womanhood for millions of Americans.

Selznick had had the foresight to put a clause in her *Intermezzo* contract that bound her to him for seven years with an option to be exercised by the mutual agreement of both parties after the film opened. Within days of the opening, Selznick exercised the option and Bergman agreed.

Selznick didn't have anything immediately ready for her, so she first did a Broadway play. Then she was lent out for a series of films, including *Rage in Heaven* in which she played the unfortunate young wife of a crazed Robert Montgomery. Then came the film that would make her immortal.

Jack Warner was desperately looking for a young European heroine for *Casablanca*. Several actresses had turned down the role, but Bergman agreed. While her acting performance was not much more than adequate, she got caught up in the tremendous commercial success of the film. Suddenly she became a hot property.

At the time when *Casablanca* opened, Paramount was facing another disaster. Ernest Hemingway had originally wanted Bergman to play opposite Gary Cooper in *For Whom The Bell Tolls*. The studio thought Bergman was not well known enough, so they cast actress Vera Zorina instead. The first rushes from the shoot told them they had made a big mistake. Zorina was dreadful. They begged Bergman to take over the part. She did, and when the film went on to be a blockbuster, her career was firmly launched.

Ingrid Bergman saved *For Whom The Bell Tolls*. She proved to have an uncanny knack of pulling movie projects out of trouble.

Paramount had commissioned a script for Irene Dunne about a frightened, frail housewife being driven crazy by her domineering husband. When Dunne turned it down, Paramount sold the script to MGM. MGM renamed it *Gaslight* and put Charles Boyer in as the husband and Hedy Lamarr as the wife. Shortly before filming was due to start, Lamarr backed out. Capitalizing on Bergman's new popularity, MGM signed her for the role. She went on to win the Best Actress Oscar for her performance.

Another unpromising project she took on was *Saratoga Trunk* in a role both Bette Davis and Vivien Leigh had (wisely) turned down. This one was beyond redemption. One modern critic calls it 'unbearable at times'. Nonetheless, Ingrid Bergman was a smashing success. The only problem was that she still hadn't made a picture for Selznick after *Intermezzo*. Selznick decided to remedy the situation.

He had just agreed to produce Alfred Hitchcock's next two movies. He wanted his 'Swedish Sensation' to be in both of them. Hitchcock certainly had no objections. The first of the two films was *Spellbound* in which Bergman played a psychiatrist in love with her patient, Gregory Peck. The second was *Notorious* with Cary Grant. *Notorious* had to be held up while Grant finished *Night and Day*.

In the meantime, against his better judgment (he thought she was being overworked), Selznick lent Bergman to RKO where she starred opposite Bing Crosby in *The Bells of St Mary's* (Crosby had just won the Oscar for *Going My Way*, which also earned Best Picture).

The *Notorious* script had Cary Grant as the character Devlin, a sharp sophisticated, nearly sadistic American counterspy. Bergman played Alicia, a nymphomaniac and the emotionally unstable daughter of a convicted Nazi spy. Devlin must recruit her to work for him to trap a master Nazi spy, Alexander Sebastian, played by Claude Rains. What Devlin does not realize will happen, of course, is that he falls in love with Alicia, and then has to order her to seduce the Nazi. Sebastian, in turn, also falls in love with Alicia and asks her to marry him. Alicia must either marry the Nazi or give up the mission. Devlin has to decide which is more important to him: Alicia, or the trapping of Sebastian.

Hitchcock had been wanting to make the film for several years, ever since Selznick had shown him a *Saturday Evening Post* story about an actress, a counterspy, who goes to bed with a spy and then worries that it will ruin her prospects for marriage. He didn't particularly like the story itself but loved the Mata Hari idea of a woman using sex to get information from a spy. He took the premise to writer Ben Hecht to work up a script.

Hecht and Hitchcock had two very different ideas about what the film was supposed to be. Hitchcock saw it as a love story. From the very beginning, he intended to make *Notorious* as sensual and erotic as the censors would allow. Hecht saw the movie as a sharp spy drama. He wrote a brilliant script along those lines. When Hitchcock saw Hecht's finished script, genius that he was, he realized immediately that he could have his cake and eat it, too. He could concentrate on the mood, while the script told the story.

Selznick refused the idea. Do one or the other, he said. He didn't understand Hitchcock's concept, and if *he* didn't, it was unlikely that the ticket-buying public would either. He was ready to abandon the whole thing. Then Hitchcock went to dinner with William Dozier, a production executive at RKO. Hitchcock told Dozier about *Notorious* and Dozier got excited. He called Selznick and made him an offer.

In a burst of colossally bad judgment, Selznick sold the entire project, script, cast and director, to RKO for $800,000 and half the profits. Since those profits eventually came to more than $10 million, it was not one of Selznick's better decisions. Later on, Hitchcock said, 'I thought it was quite silly of him.'

Once again in the hands of the master, Grant turned in a magnificent performance. At first charmingly manipulative, he gets sulky and small-minded when his new love (of Bergman) is not returned. As one critic put it, 'He reaches levels of mean-spiritedness that from any other leading man would startle an audience, but which from Cary Grant are almost devastating.'

The *New York Times* said it 'was just about as thrilling as they come with an intensity of warm emotional appeal'. Another critic wrote, 'Cary Grant brings glamour and sultry vitality to the lead.' Many critics would come to name *Notorious* as perhaps *the* outstanding performance of Cary Grant's career.

What with the war, his problems with Barbara Hutton and his heavy work schedule, Grant hadn't returned to England to see his mother, now almost 70, for some time. When *Notorious* was completed in February, he decided to sail for England, both to see Elsie and to look at the possibility of working in the newly rebuilt British film industry.

Elsie had come through the war well, although she had missed her only son. In an interview with a Bristol newspaper just before his visit, she confided, 'It's been a long time since I have seen him but he writes regularly and I see all his films. But I wish he would settle down and raise a family. That would be a great relief for me.' Mothers never change.

When he arrived, Elsie had a surprise for him. During the war she had acquired a cocker spaniel that she had named 'Cary'. Could her son perhaps get the dog into pictures? After all, she reminded him, he had done so well with that dog, Asta, in *The Awful Truth* and her Cary was just as smart.

With visiting in Bristol and talking to London producers, the stay in England lasted for some time. Grant realized that he missed England and promised himself more time there every year. He talked about buying a home in London and perhaps making one picture a year there. While he was in London, *Notorious* opened. It did record sales at Radio City Music Hall. Both *Night and Day* and *Notorious* were making tons of money at the same time.

When Grant got back to Hollywood in late June, he immediately had a phone call from Selznick. Selznick had a problem. The now teenaged Shirley Temple was still under contract and desperately needed a film that would transform her from a child star into an adolescent. The assignment was given to a then unknown screenwriter, Sidney Sheldon.

Using Sheldon's idea, Temple would be a high-school girl with a crush on her teacher whom she lures into a compromising situation. This results in a trial, with a judge sentencing the teacher either to go to jail or to be the girl's escort until she gets tired of him and starts to look at young men of her own age.

Myrna Loy, without regard to how much older she was than Temple, agreed to play Shirley's level-headed older sister, who 'coincidentally' is a judge and who 'coincidentally' is given her sister's case to try. Selznick thought he needed a guaranteed box-office draw to play the teacher, to make sure the public would come to see the grown-up Shirley Temple. Would Grant take the role as a favour? He certainly would.

After the hard work of *Notorious*, *The Bachelor and the Bobby-Soxer* was just plain fun to make. In one scene, Grant is teaching his class, dressed in a conservative business suit. Temple starts daydreaming and suddenly he's teaching dressed in a full suit of armour. He got up to all sorts of tricks, doing juvenile things like running a three-legged race with Rudy Vallee as his partner. It was pure lightheartedness, and it was pure 'Cary Grant'.

The Bachelor and the Bobby-Soxer was released in 1947 and was an instant hit. The Bing Crosby/Bob Hope classic *The Road to Rio* opened at the same time, and many critics thought *Bachelor* was the funnier of the two. One critic said, 'Cary Grant has now developed a characterization that is constant, foolproof, engaging, hardy and warranted to be attractive. The audience laughed so hard I missed some of the lines.' The movie gave Shirley Temple a second career. It even went on, unbelievably, to win an Academy Award for Sheldon and to launch his career as a screenwriter.

The next thing to happen to Grant was the first of his 'deaths'. For at least two days, America thought it had lost him.

He and his friend, Howard Hughes, had flown alone to New York to test the Constellation, one of Hughes' new planes. On the way back to California, on a whim, they decided to make a detour to Mexico for a few days of fun in the sun. Without telling anyone, they changed their flight plan, ending up at a small house Hughes owned on the Mexican coast. They were both very amused when they heard the news reports of their disappearance and supposed death, after a reporter finally tracked them down.

Cary Grant's ability to fill movie theatres was putting him in great demand. Hitchcock wanted to redo *Hamlet* as a modern-day thriller and asked Grant to star in it. He thought the role was too heavy for him and turned it down.

Then he had a talk with Sam Goldwyn about a comedy he was planning to produce for RKO. It was the story of an angel who comes down from heaven to help an overworked Protestant bishop raise money for a new church and, incidentally, to help save his marriage. Goldwyn had already signed David Niven to play the bishop and Loretta Young to play his wife. Would Grant be interested in playing Dudley, the angel? Yes, he would. They agreed to meet to discuss details.

Up to this point, just about every deal Grant signed was negotiated by his agent, Frank Vincent. But Vincent was in hospital. This time, Grant would negotiate for himself. His demand was simple, and staggering: top billing and a guaranteed $300,000 against a percentage of the profits. He himself was probably a little taken aback when Goldwyn, knowing the earnings of Grant's last three films, gulped and agreed.

The deal was signed before Grant saw the final script. When he did, he wasn't happy. The script for *The Bishop's Wife* was supposed to have been written by Robert Sherwood. Sherwood had won several Pulitzer Prizes and an Academy Award. He had written the screenplay for Hitchcock's highly acclaimed *Rebecca*. He was greatly respected. But Sherwood and Goldwyn had argued, and Goldwyn turned the project over to a series of writers. Once again, it was script-by-committee, a no-win proposition.

To add fuel to the flame, after filming started, Goldwyn had a falling-out with the director, William Seiter. He fired Seiter and replaced him with Henry Koster. Koster not only threw out the script but also the sets and costumes and anything else he could find. He started again from scratch. The film was already booked into cinemas for Christmas, so everyone went into a whirlwind to get it finished.

Convinced that he had become involved in Tinseltown's answer to the *Titanic*, Grant went to Goldwyn and offered him all his money back if he would let him out of the picture. Goldwyn panicked. The changes in director, script and sets were said already to have cost him over $900,000. If his most bankable star walked off the set, he stood to lose his Christmas cinema bookings (and possibly his shirt). Goldwyn made a quick counter-offer. He would give Grant a $100,000 rise if he would stay with the film. Grant agreed. His now-$400,000 guarantee was believed to be the largest up-front money ever paid to an actor until that time.

They finished shooting the picture, but no one was thrilled with the result. Goldwyn showed it to several test audiences. They all hated it. In desperation, he called his friend Billy Wilder. Would Wilder help?

Another Hollywood legend began. Wilder watched the movie. He told Goldwyn he was right. It was horrible. But he thought he could help. The story goes that he started writing fast and furious on Friday night. He kept on writing all day Saturday, then into Saturday night. Sunday came and he kept writing – right up until Monday morning. All in all, he wrote four brand new scenes and rewrote several others. On Monday morning, the cast and crew were called back to the set and the new and revised scenes were shot. The film was re-edited and *The Bishop's Wife* opened in time for Christmas.

The critics didn't take it too seriously. Most said it was amusing. A typical review read, 'This fantasy will probably entertain you and put you in gay Christmas spirits. However, if you have read Robert Nathan's book (on which the film was based) you will probably be disappointed.' Once again, Grant's work was singled out. 'It is Cary Grant's playing that rescues the role of the angel named Dudley from the ultimate peril of coyness. With nothing more than a beaming countenance and an air of relaxation that is certainly not of this world, he achieves a celestial manner without so much as a hint of wings on his dark blue suit.'

At this point, you could probably have made a movie about the moulting patterns of chickens in Kansas and so long as you put Cary Grant's name on the bill, you'd sell tickets. *The Bishop's Wife* was only a so-so movie, but with Cary Grant as top billing, audiences crowded into the cinemas.

Even given all the money this movie cost to make, Goldwyn managed to make a nice profit. Cary Grant's reputation as box-office gold was growing. He now had six blockbusters in a row. He had received the record $400,000 for *The Bishop's Wife*. His minimum guarantee per film was now $150,000. Even more importantly for him, Grant had won ecstatic reviews for both serious roles and light-hearted comedies. He was back on top. His cure of going back to work had done the trick. He had fully recovered from his bout of depression. His failed marriage to Barbara Hutton and his hurt over the Oscars were behind him.

8

MIDDLE YEARS

CARY GRANT HAD ALMOST three months free before he was due to start his next picture, so he decided to visit England again. He would see his mother and talk more with British producers about possible projects.

At this point, one of Grant's closest friends was the English author and playwright, Freddie Lonsdale. Lonsdale had spent most of the Second World War in the US, either living in New York or with Grant in Santa Monica. Lonsdale wanted to go home also, so the two set off on what was planned to be about a month-long visit.

They had a great time. Grant stayed in London and made frequent trips to Bristol to see his mother. In London, he and Freddie went to a party or to the theatre every night. Twice they went to see the hit show of that season, *Deep Are The Roots*, starring a slight, dark-haired young American actress, Betsy Drake. On both occasions, Grant remarked to Lonsdale how attracted he was to her.

He would soon be due back in California to start his next film, but he wanted to stretch out the holiday a little. Instead of flying as originally planned, he and Lonsdale booked passage on the *Queen Elizabeth*, and set sail from Plymouth in early September.

This was still the era of great Atlantic Crossings, with glamorous people and lush surroundings. As they were coming on board, they met Elizabeth Taylor, who was travelling with her mother. She asked Grant to dine with them the first night out because her mother was a great fan of his. He accepted with pleasure.

The ship sailed into rough seas and there was some tossing around. As he was on his way to the first-class dining-room, he held the door open for some people behind him. Just then the ship took a big lurch and a young woman was all but thrown into his arms. It was Betsy Drake, the 24-year-old American whom he had liked so much in the play. She apologized for her clumsiness and hurried off before he could get more than a few words out.

Grant was now determined to meet her. The next day he sent his friend, the actress Merle Oberon, up to Betsy to ask her to join them for lunch. He later said, 'I told Merle to go tell Betsy she had to have lunch with a lonely man. She said she would be delighted.'

They were inseparable for the remainder of the trip. Betsy told him her life story. Her father had built Chicago's famous Drake Hotel, but lost all his money in the stock market crash. Her parents divorced when she was nine. She had gone to London after failing to get a screen test in Hollywood and had taken various stage roles, ending with *Deep Are The Roots*. Now she was going home to try either Broadway or maybe Hollywood, but probably Broadway first.

Before the ship docked in New York, Grant had offered to take Betsy to Hollywood and help her break into films. He explained that he was signed to make a film for RKO called *Every Girl Should Be Married*. There was a role in it for which she'd be perfect. She said she would think about it, but first had to see a number of Broadway producers about possible plays. They parted in New York, Betsy to stay for her meetings, Grant to return to California to begin his next film.

Back in Hollywood, Grant started work at RKO on *Mr Blandings Builds His Dream House* with Myrna Loy and Melvyn Douglas. This was a light-hearted comedy about a New York advertising man who decides that it is time to move his wife and daughters to the suburbs. He buys an old house only to find it is a disaster. All he can do is tear it down and build a new one. This begins the war of wills between Mr Blandings

(Grant) and the builder and his men. The project gets more and more expensive and now he has to resist the impulses of his 'cost-is-no-object' wife. He demands that the plans be scaled back. She refuses. One such test of wills ends in Loy's famous line, 'I will not endanger the health of my children in a house with less than three bathrooms.'

Anyone who had ever owned a house or tried to build one could identify with this story. Grant was wonderful as the exasperated advertising executive. A critic called his James Blandings 'one of Grant's most effortlessly expert portrayals'. A modern critic described the movie as a 'slick-comedy . . . expertly handled'.

During the filming of *Mr Blandings*, Betsy called to ask if his offer of help was still open. She wasn't interested in any of the possibilities open to her on Broadway. She thought that now was the time to take a stab at the movies. Grant assured her that his offer was genuine and that he honestly thought she would be perfect for his next film. Betsy came to Hollywood and found herself an apartment.

As soon as she arrived, Grant introduced her to both David O. Selznick and Dore Schary, RKO's head of production. They tested her and agreed to cast her opposite Grant in *Every Girl Should Be Married*. This was the last picture he owed RKO under his current contract. RKO agreed to Betsy partly because her screen test was really pretty good, and partly because they wanted to keep Grant happy. By now he was RKO's biggest box-office draw, not to mention a close friend of the man who had just bought the studio, Howard Hughes.

Every Girl is the familiar story of a poor young woman (Drake), this time a salesgirl in a department store, who schemes to catch an older, elegant bachelor (Grant), this time a doctor. It certainly wasn't a memorable film, but it was well-made and well-acted. Both critics and the public liked it.

Betsy even got good reviews, with *Newsweek* writing, 'Most responsible for making it funny is a gangling, effervescent lass named Betsy Drake, whose previous film experience amounts to a Hollywood screen test.' Several critics predicted a successful career for her. The film made money, too. It earned RKO almost a million dollars, which made Selznick very happy.

Having Betsy on the set made filming *Every Girl* a pleasant experience for Grant, and being together every day brought the couple closer.

Hollywood was undergoing a change. Productions were leaving the sound stages and going on location. In the past, only the most lavish productions had done so. Usually they were only those films that needed outdoor settings. But realism had become the new watchword of the day. More and more films were heading for exotic or faraway locales. Grant's next project followed suit.

When the filming of *Every Girl* was over, Grant left for Germany to begin working with Howard Hawks on *I Was a Male War Bride*. This is a delightful comedy about an American WAC officer, played by Ann Sheridan, who meets an egotistical, stuffy French army officer, played by Grant. At first she hates him, but eventually falls in love and marries him, only to find her troubles just beginning. Under military regulations, he cannot live in the WAC quarters and she cannot live in the French officer's quarters. Then they find that the only way the new husband can return to America is to enter under a quota for 'war brides'.

In some of the key scenes, Grant was supposed to put on a wig and a WAC uniform and play the scene in drag. In *Hawks on Hawks* by Joseph McBride (University of California Press, 1982), Hawks remembers that he and Grant had some differences at first about how those scenes should be played:

'Cary was going to put on the woman's uniform and be feminine. And he practised little tricks, worked on them and everything. And I said, "Hey don't work on it. We're not going to do that." "What do you mean?" "Well," I said, "just act like a man in women's clothing." "Oh, you're missing something there, Howard." By now we had gotten to Germany and the generals gave us a party. I got on a WAC's uniform and a red wig and let me tell you that I looked funnier than Grant did. I came in, pulled out a cigar and said, "Got a light, general?" He didn't know who I was or what I was. He thought I was a WAC. Cary was having convulsions, and he said, "You've sold me, that's how I'm going to do it."'

Betsy and Cary had started living together not long after *Every Girl Should Be Married* finished shooting. So she came with him when he left for Germany. They stopped in England to visit his mother. Elsie was delighted to meet Betsy. She still wanted him to be married and she didn't much care for his playboy image. Every time she saw him, she reminded him sternly that it was time he settled down. Now, in Betsy, she saw the possibility it would happen.

Once in Germany, shooting did not go well. The weather was horrible. Ann Sheridan, the leading lady, caught pneumonia. Then several members of the cast and crew caught jaundice. In November, they all left Germany for London, to shoot the interior scenes. Grant began to complain that he was not feeling well either. Within days, he was diagnosed as having caught jaundice.

He was seriously ill for several weeks, confined to his bed. Betsy nursed him the whole time. He was deeply grateful for her attention and began to think that perhaps he had finally found a woman who was willing to devote herself to him.

While he was sick, *Every Girl* opened in New York. There were both good reviews and long queues at the box office. It was another hit for Cary Grant. The news cheered them both up.

Male War Bride could not be filmed while Grant was ill. It was costing Hawks almost $4,000 a day to keep the project open. He decided to shelve it temporarily and to finish it back in Hollywood when Grant was healthy again. It took another month until Grant was even well enough to travel back to California. He decided to go slowly by ship, the long way directly to Los Angeles. He took a stateroom on the Holland-America ship, *Dalerdyck*, for the nearly three-week long voyage.

Betsy saw him off and then flew back to California to reopen the house for him. On the day the ship tied up in Los Angeles, she was there to meet him. So was a crowd of reporters. His illness had been a front-page story for weeks. Despite hours in the sun aboard ship, he still looked pale and wan. He had been ill for over four months and had lost more than forty pounds. The reporters, though, had only one question, 'When are you going to get married, Mr Grant?'

After another month of California sun, Grant finally felt well enough to complete the final scenes for *Male War Bride*. The effort took its toll. He was exhausted and still ill. Two days after he finished the film, he flew to Baltimore and checked himself into Johns Hopkins Hospital medical centre where he stayed for two weeks of rest and tests.

Before he left Baltimore, Hawks called to ask him to come to New York for the opening of *Male War Bride*. Grant had not seen the final cut. He was curious to see how it had come out after all the difficulties they had in filming it. Also, Hawks had had problems in the editing room. The story's entire premise was the trouble this couple had in getting into bed with one another. Even though they were married, the censors had put up a lot of objections, and Hawks had to edit around the objections.

Grant went to New York and the premiere. He was frankly surprised. He had expected not to like the finished product, but in fact loved what he saw. The day after the premiere, he told *The New York Times*, 'I just saw the picture and the audience laughed themselves sick. I've been in many comedies but I've never heard an audience react like this one. I honestly feel its the best comedy I've ever done.' That might have been an overstatement, but the public certainly loved it. The movie grossed over $4.5 million and was 20th Century-Fox's biggest hit of the year.

Grant went back to California in September with his mind made up. He would marry Betsy as soon as she liked. She wanted to get married, but she also wanted to continue her own career. Her reviews for *Every Girl*, and its commercial success, had brought her several offers. She had accepted two projects. Grant agreed to delay the marriage until they were finished.

Betsy started work on *Pretty Baby* for Jack Warner with co-star Edmund Gwenn. Grant was still weak from his illness. He was more than happy to take a few more months off to lie in the sun and wait for Betsy to finish her commitments. They thought they'd be able to get married sometime in the spring. Christmas was approaching, and Grant was spending his time lolling around the house. His friend Howard Hughes decided things had gone on long enough. He told Cary and Betsy he was taking them away to celebrate the holiday.

On Christmas Day, 1949, Hughes picked them up and flew them to Phoenix, Arizona, to one of Hughes' friends' homes. Within an hour and a half of touchdown, the two were married. Betsy was 26 and Cary not quite 46. Hughes was best man at the wedding. He even bought the ring. Betsy would later say she didn't have the slightest idea who attended the whirlwind celebrations.

The groom, with the third Mrs Grant, returned that night to Hollywood. Betsy immediately moved into Grant's gorgeous six-bedroom Beverly Hills home. The next morning, she returned to her apartment to gather her things. That day, Grant picked up a wedding present for his bride – a white poodle that Betsy named Suzie.

By the beginning of 1950, Cary Grant had already completed three-quarters of the films he would ever make. Having worked almost continuously over the past 17 years he had been in Hollywood, he had done 54 movies. Now, several things came together to slow down that output. For one, he was tired. The hard work of his life was catching up with him. He often told Betsy how he had always planned for his future with his money. Because of his investments, he really didn't need to work another day in his life. He talked of retirement, of sailing around the world, of spending time wherever his fancy took him.

Then too, the movie industry was changing. Films were getting longer. In the early days, it was common for movies to run around 70 minutes. Now 100-minute running times were the average. As a result, studios were spending more time and money on each film they started. No more 30-day or six-week shooting schedules. That meant movies had to run longer in cinemas to make the investment back. So there were fewer available outlets for new films and the studios made fewer each year.

Also, the studios were now worried about big-name actors having more than one film in release at a time. They didn't want an actor to be 'in competition' with himself. It wasn't that big stars like Cary Grant got fewer offers, but that once they accepted a project, other offers would be held up.

Cary Grant had one more reason for not working so much, and this was the most important one. This marriage was going to work. It was a huge priority in his life.

In early 1950, he was committed to only one picture, *Crisis*. It had been written by Richard Brooks, who had also done *Key Largo* for Humphrey Bogart.

Crisis is the story of a famous brain surgeon (Grant) on vacation in a Latin American country. He gets kidnapped to perform emergency surgery on the local dictator (Jose Ferrer). Revolutionaries kidnap the doctor's daughter and tell him he must kill the dictator on the operating table or else his daughter will die. He cannot, however, and saves the dictator. Then he saves his daughter while the dictator is killed when the revolutionaries storm the palace.

A former sports reporter, novelist and stage director, Richard Brooks had been in Hollywood for many years. He was originally hired as a contract scriptwriter by Universal and then moved on to Warner Brothers where he wrote not only the highly successful *Key Largo* but also *Crossfire*, an adaptation of his own novel.*

In 1949, MGM was in trouble. The studio had acquired the reputation of producing only glossy films of little substance. To change this, they hired Dore Schary away from RKO, where he was not getting along with Howard Hughes, to become MGM's production head.

One of Schary's first moves was to lure Brooks away from Warner Brothers. Schary wanted to start producing hard-hitting adult dramas, which was what Brooks wrote. Schary sealed the deal with the promise that Brooks would be allowed to direct.

---

* Brooks' later credits include his novel *The Producer*, published in 1951, and many popular movies, including *The Blackboard Jungle* (1955), *Cat on a Hot Tin Roof* (1958), *Lord Jim* (1965), *In Cold Blood* (1967), and *Looking for Mr Goodbar* (1977).

Brooks' first finished script at MGM was *Crisis*. He was determined to make it his directing debut. Schary had sent a copy of the script to Grant, who liked it. Grant called Brooks, who he knew from the race-track. He asked if the scriptwriter was the same Richard Brooks he knew from Santa Anita. Brooks assured him this was so.

Brooks asked Grant what he thought of the script. Grant said he liked it and might be willing to do it. Next came Brooks' key question. He knew that Grant had director approval on all his films. Would Grant consider letting him direct? Sure, said Grant. He liked Brooks, and besides, who could better understand a script than its writer?

Giving Brooks the chance to direct for the first time points up one of the big contradictions in Cary Grant's professional life. He was known to be a perfectionist, someone who would quibble and argue over the smallest detail in any film he was in. He had a reputation for being a hard man to work with unless you were Howard Hawks or Alfred Hitchcock or, by now, Leo McCarey, all of whom he trusted. However, he always seemed to be open to working with a first-time director.

Delmer Daves remembers how Grant gave him his first directing job in 1943. 'As a writer, I had been working at sea in submarines to get the technical details right for the final script on *Destination Tokyo*. Jack Warner was concerned that his director understand the technical details of submarines so he asked if I would direct. I said yes immediately.

'The producer was Jerry Wald and he had sent a copy of the script to Cary. Grant called to say he approved the script. He asked who the director was going to be. Wald, in fear and trembling because he knew that Cary had director approval, said, "Delmer Daves." Cary hesitated a bit, thought it over and then said, "Why yes, Delmer Daves would make a fine director."

'So Wald called Warner and said that Cary had approved me as director. Then not ten minutes later, Grant's agent called and said he had heard that Cary wanted to do *Destination Tokyo*. "Who was going to direct?" he asked. Wald said, "Delmer Daves". "He has never directed a picture in his life. You want him to direct Cary Grant? I won't allow it. I refuse to allow a new man who has never directed to direct Cary.'' Wald said OK and called Warner back to tell him that he had better find a director. That seemed to be the end of it but a few minutes later the agent called back to say the only way Cary would make the film was if Delmer Daves directed it.

'Later I asked Cary why he had stuck by me. He said he had known me as a friend, had liked many of the pictures I had written and felt I would make a good director. ''Why shouldn't I be the first to say I have faith in Delmer Daves?'' he said.'

The distinguished Puerto Rican-born actor, Jose Ferrer, was signed to play the dictator. With Grant in the lead, part of the script had to be reworked. As originally written, the doctor was to be a widower with a nine-year-old daughter who is held hostage until the operation was successfully botched. Dore Schary did not want Grant to be without a love interest, so the daughter was changed into a wife, played by Helen Ferguson.

When shooting was complete, Cary and Betsy moved into a house in Palm Springs, a home they grew to love. *Crisis* opened to generally favourable reviews. Grant in particular got good notices for his work. One reviewer said, 'Cary Grant is more brittle and diamond-brilliant than before as the enlightened doctor. His sincerity in the story's guts is its premise for being believed.' Another wrote, 'Both Grant and Ferrer are superlative – but even these seasoned actors take on new dimensions with Brooks' telling them how to do it.'

As frequently seems to happen, the critics and the public didn't agree. *Crisis* did not do well at the box-office. It was Cary Grant's first commercial failure in many pictures but he really didn't care.

For the rest of the year he and Betsy remained in Palm Springs or travelled. He didn't even bother to read the scripts that arrived in a steady stream. His only foray into the entertainment business was a radio drama with Irene Dunne that Betsy had written. It was based on *Mr Blandings Builds His Dream House*. It was not a big success, but since it made Betsy happy, he was glad to do it.

Not many people realize how much radio Grant did over the

years. Starting in the mid-1930s, he was a regular on radio dramas, many done for the Lux Radio Theatre sponsored by Lever Brothers. Quite often the radio dramas were recreations of his films with the same casts. *The Philadelphia Story* with Jimmy Stewart and Kate Hepburn (1942), *The Talk of the Town* with Ronald Colman and Jean Arthur (1943), and *Every Girl Should Be Married* with Betsy are examples.

At the beginning of 1951, Grant was tempted back to the movies by a project of Joseph Mankiewicz'. Mankiewicz, an American, had arrived in Hollywood in the late 1920s from Berlin, where he and his brother Herman had been correspondents. He started as a screenwriter and producer. In 1946, he was given a chance to direct *Dragonwyck* and turned out to be one of Hollywood's most intelligent and literate directors. He was known for his witty scripts and fast, often sarcastic dialogue.

In 1949, Mankiewicz won the Best Director and Best Screenplay Oscars for *A Letter to Three Wives*, which was also nominated for Best Picture. In 1950, he again won the Academy Awards for Best Director and Screenplay for *All About Eve* which dominated the Oscars that year. Mankiewicz wanted to follow up *All About Eve* with *People Will Talk* starring Cary Grant. Grant couldn't pass up the opportunity. He agreed.

It was not to be one of Cary Grant's more memorable outings although the film was well made, and Grant did his usual competent job. *Newsweek* called it 'one of the most intelligent performances in his 19-year Hollywood career'. But the role itself was a disaster.

Dr Noah Praetorius, as Grant's character was named, was a gynaecologist. He marries a pregnant patient to keep her from either having an abortion or committing suicide. When he was not delivering perfect babies, he was saving souls or conducting a symphony orchestra, and conducting it very well. As one critic said, 'He (Grant) moved up from an angel to a saint.' It was one of the rare movies in which Grant was actually unlikeable. Even he could not overcome the smugness of Mankiewicz' writing.

The film had significant political overtones. The early 1950s were the time of the McCarthy communist witch-hunts in Washington. Mankiewicz had himself just won the presidency of the Screen Director's Guild against a right-wing slate headed by Cecil B. De Mille. In *People Will Talk*, Dr Praetorius is subjected to and overcomes an official inquiry headed by the right-wing Dr Elwell (Hume Cronyn).

On the heels of *Crisis*, this was Grant's second box-office failure in a row.

While Cary and Betsy had been in Palm Springs, they had talked about doing another film together. Selznick called with an offer for Grant to do Scott Fitzgerald's *Tender Is the Night* with Jennifer Jones and directed by George Cukor, but he said no. Warner Brothers and Howard Hawks wanted him to star in a remake of *Don Quixote*, with the Mexican actor, Cantinflas, as Sancho Panza. He expressed some interest, but the project never got off the ground.

Jack Warner asked if there was any particular project he wanted to do. He replied, 'Something with Betsy'. So Warner Brothers went out and found a script they thought would suit the two of them. It was called *Room For One More*.

The story had a financially hard-pressed city employee (Grant) with a heart-of-gold wife (Drake). The couple take in five unwanted children. Betsy loved the script, so he agreed to do it. Grant received ten per cent of the film's gross revenues with a guarantee of $100,000. Betsy was paid $25,000.

Grant probably enjoyed making the film more than any other in recent years. With Betsy there, he seemed to love every day on the set. When *Room For One More* was released, reviewers called it 'a delightful domestic comedy'. While it did respectable business in the box office, it didn't come close to many of Grant's earlier hits. (The movie was later retitled *The Easy Way*, and became the basis for a TV show.)

While making *Room for One More*, possibly because he was in a very happy frame of mind, he agreed to do two more films, one for Howard Hawks and one for Dore Schary at MGM. Both were to be old-fashioned comedies.

The Hawks film was *Monkey Business*. It was the story of a scientist who discovers a way to become young again. The youth serum makes him act like a teenager. Grant's co-star in *Monkey Business* was Ginger Rogers. She played his wife, who also drinks the youth serum. In fact, Grant also gets his boss, played by Charles Coburn, and his secretary to drink it. That secretary was Marilyn Monroe in one of her first film appearances.

As Howard Hawks remembered it, 'Marilyn Monroe was the most frightened little girl who had no confidence in her ability. She was afraid to come on the screen. Very strange girl . . . But when she got out in front of the camera, the camera liked her, suddenly she was a great sex symbol. I was lucky to work with her early, before she became frightened. Cary was a lot of help with her in *Monkey Business*. She seemed to listen to him. But I had an easy time compared to other directors who worked with her later. The more important she became the more frightened she became.'

The other comedy Cary Grant did at this time was *Dream Wife* for MGM. Written by Sidney Sheldon, it was an attempt to cash in on the success of *The Bachelor and the Bobby-Soxer*. Starring Deborah Kerr, Walter Pidgeon and Buddy Baer, *Dream Wife* was a silly bedroom comedy about Grant 'marrying' an Eastern princess for goodwill reasons. Modern critics say the 'cast was wasted'.

Around the same time he took on the two comedies, Grant turned down a number of more serious roles. These included the one that went to Gregory Peck opposite Audrey Hepburn in *Roman Holiday*.

At one point George Cukor went to Palm Springs to try to persuade Grant to act opposite Judy Garland in the new version of *A Star Is Born*, the story of an ageing actor whose young wife is about to become a star. Cukor wrote that he and Grant sat around the pool and Grant read from a portion of the new script. For years afterwards Cukor swore that Grant's reading that day was the finest thing he ever seen the actor do, and much better than anything that James Mason eventually did in the role. He begged Grant to take the part, pleading that he was perfect for it. But Grant said no.

With the failures of *Crisis* and *People Will Talk* he was again shying away from roles. Once again, he was unsure of himself as an actor.

In doing light comedy, Grant was bucking a trend in Hollywood. Studios were turning out heavy dramas like *Death of a Salesman* and *Come Back, Little Sheba*, or adventures like *High Noon*. Light comedies were getting lost in the shuffle and, not too surprisingly, both *Monkey Business* and *Dream Wife* were failures. *Monkey Business* actually got quite a few good reviews, but the public just did not want to see comedies.

This was even more evident when *Dream Wife* opened in June 1952. The reviewers said nice things about both Grant and Deborah Kerr, but dismissed the film almost out of hand. This was the era of 'significant' films. The public stayed away in droves.

For the first and only time in his 30-year career, Cary Grant had suffered four box-office flops in a row. For the last two years, he had talked more and more seriously about retiring. The failures of his last films confirmed for him that Hollywood had changed and there wasn't room any more for the kind of movies Cary Grant made. Twenty years after he was 'born', it looked as if it was time to retire 'Cary Grant'. In mid-1953, a few weeks after *Dream Wife* opened, Grant announced his retirement.

9

BACK ON TOP

CARY GRANT WAS NEARLY 50 years old. He had retired from show business. He decided the movie industry had gone beyond him.

He later wrote, 'It was the period of blue jeans and dope addicts and the "Method" and nobody cared about comedy at all.' He would do what he had been saying for years he wanted to do, simply travel the world with the woman he loved. He and Betsy began a round-the-world cruise by tramp steamer, sailing from San Francisco for Japan. From there they went on to India; then around the Horn of Africa to Europe, and eventually to England and another long visit with Elsie.

Betsy loved reading and their cabin was crowded with her books. She was also an excellent amateur photographer and took pictures everywhere they went with a new set of cameras Cary had given her. At almost every port of call, he was met by reporters who would ask if he was really retired. Yes, he would insist, yes he was.

Betsy got into things like fad diets, yoga and self-hypnotism. During the trip they went on various kinds of diets and exercise programmes. She got Grant to give up his habit of three packs of cigarettes a day by using self-hypnosis. He used to tell the story often: 'I planted a post-hypnotic suggestion that I stop smoking. I went to sleep and the next morning when I arose the first thing I did, as I always did, was to light up a cigarette. I took one puff and I was instantly nauseated. I put it out and have never lit one since.'

When they got back to Palm Springs, Cary Grant was happy and more rested than he had been for years. It was Christmas, and Betsy and Cary did some entertaining. Basically though, they continued the lifestyle they had adopted before their trip. They spent time alone, he in the sun, she reading or carrying on one of her many hobbies.

Not long after his birthday on January 18, he started to get restless. He began to make trips into Hollywood to see his friends and people at the studios. It had been more than a year since he finished shooting *Dream Wife*. He began to realize that he missed working.

Over the months that followed his return from his trip around the world, people had continued to call with projects and offers. Scripts continued to arrive, but he rejected them pretty much out of hand. One of the roles he turned down was given to William Holden. It was in the Oscar-winning *The Bridge on the River Kwai*. Grant started to think that if exactly the right project came along, he might go back to work.

About that time, executives at RKO were trying to persuade Alfred Hitchcock to do a film based on a novel they had optioned several years earlier, *To Catch a Thief*, by David Dodge. Set in the French Riviera, the story was about a reformed jewel thief, John Robie, who comes under suspicion when a new series of robberies starts occurring which carries his trademark. The only way to clear his name is to catch the real thief.

Hitchcock liked the story. He had just completed *Rear Window* with Jimmy Stewart. The idea of a comedy-thriller was appealing after such a heavy drama. Even more, he loved the Riviera. He probably would have made just about any picture that was going to be shot on location in the South of France. The fact that he actually liked the story was icing on the cake.

Hitchcock knew exactly who he wanted for the character Frances Stevens, John Robie's love interest. He had discovered the young blonde Grace Kelly in a forgettable black and white feature. Her performance had impressed him, so he signed her for the lead in *Dial 'M' For Murder*. She was his ideal leading lady. She had everything he looked for: a heart of fire under a cool, blonde exterior. As far as he was concerned, she was not only extremely talented, but also the easiest actress he had ever directed. He had put her into his next film, *Rear Window*, and now wanted her for *To Catch a Thief*.

Grace Kelly had commitments for three other films after *Rear Window*. She wouldn't be available to start work in France until at least June. That didn't bother Hitchcock. It gave him time to work on the script and more time to work on the man he knew should play John Robie. That man was in what Hitchcock knew to be premature retirement.

Hitchcock travelled to Palm Springs to tell Grant about the project. Hitchcock said he thought the film could be a major hit. He said the part of Robie read as if it had been written for Grant. He begged him to return to work.

It was unlikely that he had to beg all that hard. Grant had just seen *Rear Window* and loved it. He probably wished it had been him and not Jimmy Stewart sitting in the wheelchair. He had also been very impressed with Grace Kelly, both in *Rear Window* and in *Dial 'M' For Murder*.

When Hitchcock told him Kelly had agreed to co-star in the new film, Grant's mind was made up. He later said, 'I really didn't want to do the film. It was only when Hitch told me I would play opposite Grace Kelly that I did accept.'

While he waited for Kelly to finish her other projects, Hitchcock went to France to shoot 'second unit' action, like the car chase scenes. With nothing else to do, Betsy and Grant left Palm Springs early and went along with Hitchcock. They all stopped in England, the Grants to see Elsie, now almost 80 but going as strong as ever, and Hitchcock and his wife Alma to see their families. It was a short but enjoyable visit. Then it was on to the Riviera where the Grants settled in while Hitchcock worked. By the time Kelly arrived and the main shooting started, Grant was rested, happy and in a perfect frame of mind to resume work.

This spirit of relaxation carried over into the filming. On this set, the actors and the director were like a family. Kelly had been a little tired when she arrived from California but she perked up immediately when she met the local prince, a man named Rainier. Above all, Hitchcock was his usual self. He told the actors what he wanted and then got out of the way.

Much of the action and even many of the lines were improvised. For example, Kelly unexpectedly kissed a shocked Grant square on the lips in a shot that simply called for them to walk down a hotel corridor together. This took place so early in the shooting that they were barely on a first-name basis. There was a sexual undercurrent throughout almost every scene between Grant and Kelly. Many of the lines and physical actions they improvised dripped with innuendo.

One particular exchange they improvised has become one of the most famous in film history. Grant and Kelly have gone on a picnic. She is determined to get him to confess that he is a jewel thief.

Kelly: 'I've never caught a jewel thief before. It's so stimulating. (She reaches into the picnic basket.) Do you want a breast or a leg?'

Grant: 'You make the choice.'

Kelly: 'Now tell me, how long has it been?'

Grant: 'Since what?'

Kelly: 'Since you were last in America?'

In another scene, he takes her back to her hotel suite and there is a fireworks display going on outside the large picture windows.

Kelly: 'If you really want to see fireworks, it's better with the lights off. (She moves closer in her strapless gown.) I have a feeling that tonight you're going to see some of the Riviera's most fascinating sights. (Pause.) I mean the fireworks, of course.'

Grant: 'May I have a brandy? May I fix you one?'

Kelly: (Leaning forward with the light shining off a dazzling diamond necklace.) 'Give up – admit who you are. Even in this light I can tell where you are looking. Look. Hold them. (Pause.) Diamonds.' (She takes his hand and places it underneath the necklace.) Ever have a better offer in your life?'

Grant: 'I've never had a crazier one.'

Kelly: 'Just as long as you're satisfied.'

Grant: 'You know as well as I do this necklace is imitation.'

Kelly: 'Well, I'm not.'

In the days of the Production Board censors, that kind of dialogue was nothing short of revolutionary. Hitchcock admitted that he left some of it in fully expecting it to be blue-pencilled. To his surprise, the censors left it alone. In our present world of show-all, tell-all and hear-all there are many that would argue that Grant's and Kelly's innuendo is far sexier than anything on the screen today.

Grant realized that his scenes with Kelly were among the best he had ever done. Like Hitchcock, he had expected the film to be fun to make and a good reason to go to the Riviera. But as filming progressed, both Grant and Hitchcock became very excited about the film's prospects. Grant got new life in him. He started talking about other projects he wanted to do. Everything that had soured him in the film business two years earlier was put aside or forgotten.

In late July, the cast went back to Hollywood to shoot indoor scenes and to reshoot a few that Hitchcock felt needed tightening. It was the first time Grant had been back on a Hollywood sound-stage for more than a year and a half. He found, truthfully, that it was not nearly as enjoyable as the location work had been in France.

When filming was finished in mid-August, some of the old doubts began to creep back. Betsy, he knew, clearly did not want him to jump back into film-making. She enjoyed having him at home. He also realized that at times on the Riviera, she had been resentful of his glamorous co-star. There had been several unflattering, and totally unfair, comparisons of Betsy and Grace Kelly in the French and British press.

By the time Cary and Betsy got back to Palm Springs, Grant had again resolved to approach his next project cautiously. If something exceptional like To Catch a Thief came along, he would consider it. But, he told himself, it would have to be exceptional.

As often happened to both Grant and Hitchcock, To Catch a Thief opened to mixed reviews. Variety said, 'The sad truth is this film is a disappointment. Billed as a comedy-mystery, it stacks up as a drawn-out pretentious piece that seldom hits comedy level. Grant, however, once again demonstrates he is a master of timing, getting laughs where a lesser talent would have drawn a blank.' Another critic called it a fluff film, without much social meaning, but predicted it would be a hit. 'Ten million ladies will give you Albert Schweitzer and Pandit Nehru, if they can have Cary Grant.'

Despite the reviews, as Hitchcock had promised, *To Catch a Thief* quickly became a major hit. It was one of the year's top draws. The public came out strong for Cary Grant. He was still box-office magic.

It proved something to him. He had retired after a series of failures. If *To Catch a Thief* had been less fun to make, if it had been less of a hit at the box office, it might have confirmed to him that he was finished, that time had passed him by. He probably would have gone back to retirement and never again set foot in front of the cameras. But he had fun, the movie was a hit, and much of the desire to stay retired went away.

Offers and scripts poured into Palm Springs. He remained cautious. The flamboyant Broadway producer Mike Todd came calling. Todd, who had just married Elizabeth Taylor, was being called the film industry's new P. T. Barnum. Todd told Grant about his plans to mount the most lavish film the world had ever seen. It was based on Jules Verne's *Around the World in 80 Days*. Todd said that it would be shot in every corner of the world and would feature cameo appearances by every major star in Hollywood. What he needed was a single actor to be the glue that would hold it all together. Todd offered him not only the part but a deal that would have given him partial ownership of the film and a very large part of its potentially huge profits. Grant thought it over. He finally decided it was just not his kind of film. The role went instead to David Niven.

Television was now on the scene. Grant was asked over and over again to appear on TV. He enjoyed doing radio. People said television was nothing more than radio with pictures. But Grant didn't see it that way. He liked to watch it, and often did so. But he didn't like the men who controlled the new industry. He thought they were fast-buck artists with little or no creative flair.

'I won't do television. It's silly to set myself up in competition with myself,' was his standard reply to all offers. It was a decision he never went back on.

Although still cautious, Grant was getting restless again. The restlessness was starting to affect his home-life. Both he and Betsy knew their marriage was in trouble. After talking it over, they decided the answer might be for them both to get back to work. Perhaps, they reasoned, if they were not together so much things might get better between them.

Frank Tashlin, a producer at Fox, had approached Betsy to appear in a project he was putting together. At the same time, Hollywood's hottest producer, Stanley Kramer, who had won back-to-back Oscars for *The Caine Mutiny* and *High Noon*, wanted to build his next project around Grant.

It was *The Pride and the Passion*, set in Napoleonic France. At first, Grant was not crazy about playing an English officer with long tied-back hair. It had been 15 years since the fiasco of *The Howards of Virginia*, but he still remembered what a disaster it had been. He didn't like the idea of getting into period costume. He also had his doubts about Sophia Loren who had accepted the female lead after it was rejected by Ava Gardner.

Eventually Kramer won him over. The film was to be shot entirely in Spain. They decided that Betsy would remain in Hollywood to prepare for the Fox film.

There were problems on the set in Spain. Grant got along well with Loren, in fact almost too well. He developed a crush on her. Loren was not getting along well with the film's second lead, Frank Sinatra. At the time Sinatra was not getting along with anyone. He eventually had a bitter fight with Kramer and left Spain before the film was completed. Grant had to do his final scenes, supposedly with Sinatra, with a coat-hanger serving as stand-in for the absent singer.

When Betsy finished her preparations in California, she went to Spain to visit her husband. She soon realized she was making both Grant and Loren uncomfortable. So she set sail for California to start filming the Tashlin movie, *Will Success Spoil Rock Hunter?*

Betsy's trip home was extraordinary. She had the bad luck to book passage on the *Andrea Doria*. The ship was struck by the

Swedish liner, *Stockholm*, in thick fog off the coast of Nantucket. It sank. More than 50 lives were lost. Betsy was one of the fortunate ones. She managed to get into a lifeboat before the Italian liner went down. She never floundered in the cold north Atlantic waters like so many of her fellow passengers that night. She did, however, lose all her clothing and more than a quarter of a million dollars in jewels.

The first Grant heard of his wife's near tragedy was when a telegram arrived in Spain saying she was safe on board the French liner, *Ile de France*, which had picked up her lifeboat.

Despite all the problems on the set in Spain, Cary Grant returned to Hollywood a happy man. He had been away for almost six months and thought it was great to be home. He was a little worried that Hollywood might already have forgotten his success in *To Catch a Thief*. Of course it hadn't. No sooner had he stepped off the plane than new offers started to pour in.

To Catch a Thief had been a 'stylish' comedy. *The Pride and Passion* was a drama. He thought it was time to change gears again. He started looking for either a light-hearted comedy or a low-keyed romance story. Along came an offer from Leo McCarey.

McCarey, after having been one of Hollywood's top directors for two decades, had fallen on hard times. After his serious car accident, his health had deteriorated. He had started drinking and had become addicted to pain-killing drugs. He had made only one movie in the 1950s, a terrible anti-communist film, *My Son John*, in 1952. His career was clearly in danger of being over. Most of the studios were no longer interested in the kinds of films which were his speciality.

In 1938, McCarey had made *Love Affair*, a very successful light comedy-romance with Charles Boyer and Irene Dunne. It was the story of two people, Nickie Ferrante and Terry McKay, who meet while travelling to New York, each to join the person they are going to marry. They have a brief affair, but then can't forget each other. Unknown to the other they both break their engagements. Six months later, by chance, they meet again, find neither has married, and live happily ever after.

Now, 18 years after making the original, McCarey wanted to

remake it. He had obtained a new script and had renamed it *An Affair to Remember*. Delmer Daves, who had written the original, worked on the new script, updating the dialogue and adding several new scenes. The original *Love Affair* had only been 87 minutes long. It needed to be longer for the 1950s market.

McCarey was told that he could have financial backing if, and only if, he got Cary Grant to play the lead. Grant immediately agreed to help his old friend and play Nickie. Deborah Kerr signed up to play Terry.

The old saying is, 'Everything you send into the lives of others comes back into your own.' While he would have hated to admit it, the real reason Grant took this role was to help out an old colleague. He didn't expect much from the film, but when he got on the set, something clicked. Nickie Ferrante turned out to be one of Grant's most memorable roles. Nickie was basically a disreputable playboy, but Grant played him with a constant sense of irony and humour. He also developed a certain chemistry with Kerr, which, as the expression goes, was screen magic. They had begun their screen relationship with *Dream Wife*. They came to this film feeling comfortable with one another. The screen relationship grew and grew. They were terrific together.

An Affair to Remember turned out rather unevenly. McCarey had lost much of his talent. Though the early light comedy scenes were well handled, the film began to falter as it became more serious in the second half. Grant and Kerr held it together as best they could.

McCarey has said that the difference between *Love Affair* and *An Affair to Remember* was the difference between Charles Boyer and Cary Grant. Boyer was a much more serious man. He played Nickie straightforwardly, with a sense of earnestness and vulnerability. Grant played the role with coolness and a certain detachment. His finely-honed sense of humour and his good mood showed throughout the movie. *An Affair to Remember* was much funnier than the original *Love Affair*. Also, the longer running time allowed for a slower pace which helped the comedy.

McCarey later admitted that he personally preferred the original version, but said it was a question of personal taste. He just liked the story better as straight romance. There was no arguing that the ticket-buying public vastly preferred the remake. McCarey said the reason was simply that movie-goers liked Cary Grant significantly more than they ever liked Charles Boyer. This film was the only commercial success that McCarey enjoyed among the four films he directed in the 1950s and 1960s.

Cary Grant, relaxed and more at ease than he had been for years, continued working. At the time, 20th Century-Fox was promoting the woman they called the successor to Marilyn Monroe, the well-built Jayne Mansfield. They were looking for a light comedy for her to star in and chose *Kiss Them for Me*. It was based on the novel *Shore Leave* which had been a Broadway hit, about the adventures and misadventures of three World War II Navy fliers who hit San Francisco on leave.

Fox knew they needed a sure-fire box-office superstar to ensure the success of the film. They asked Cary Grant. He liked the story and was impressed with the massive publicity build-up for Mansfield. He was also tempted by the above-average fee they were offering. He had been kicking himself for turning down *Around the World in 80 Days* which had just opened to enormous box-office business. He began to think that turning down that role along with part ownership of the film was the biggest mistake he had ever made in Hollywood.

Neither *The Pride and the Passion* nor *An Affair to Remember* had opened yet, so he couldn't know what fabulous successes they would be. He accepted producer Jerry Wald's offer and Fox's generous pay to do *Kiss Them for Me* with Mansfield.

Fox wanted the young Stanley Donen to direct. Donen had started out at the age of ten as a Broadway dancer and by the time he was sixteen was dancing with Gene Kelly in the Broadway version of *Pal Joey*. He moved into behind-the-scenes work, first as a choreographer with Kelly, and then, during the late 1940s, as the unsung director of the dance sequences for many of MGM's top musicals, including *Best Foot Forward* and *On the Town*. In 1950, he was given his first directing assignment, *Royal Wedding* with Fred Astaire. He went on to direct such musicals as *Seven Brides for Seven Brothers* and *The Pajama Game*.

In a way, it was as if he was a new director, as *Kiss Them for Me* was his first non-musical, and his first comedy.

Donen remembers well his initial meeting with Grant. 'I first met Cary in producer Jerry Wald's office at Fox. He had already agreed to do the film and while Wald wanted me to direct, it was really up to him. I was a little apprehensive but the meeting went very well. He said he had seen some of my work and wanted to work with me. By the time I arrived on the scene the film was pretty well already prepared, the script was done. It turned out to be a very easy project.'

Over the course of filming, Donen and Grant became good friends. For some time, Grant had been thinking about forming his own production company so he could own the films he was making. This was the newest thing in the film industry – stars producing their own films – and to Grant it made a lot of sense. He approached Donen about it. They ended up forming a partnership that would produce three additional films, with Grant starring and Donen directing, over the next six years.

Grant went to work on *Kiss Them for Me* almost as soon as he finished *An Affair to Remember*. All went smoothly. He liked Jayne Mansfield and Suzy Parker, a model turned actress who was the second female lead. He found Donen an easy director to work for. The film was basically a comedy but as Donen noted, it had some serious undertones: 'Yes, it was a comedy, but it was also a story of how the civilian population relates to men in the military during wartime. There was a serious side to it and Cary recognized this and played it as such.'

It wasn't one of Grant's most memorable films, but he enjoyed making it. His mood got even better during filming when *An Affair to Remember* and *The Pride and the Passion* both opened to lukewarm reviews but huge box-office popularity. Their success, especially in the face of mixed reviews, confirmed that Grant was still a major attraction. It clearly lifted his spirits.

He was still infatuated with Sophia Loren. He had been looking for a project they both could star in. He had asked a number of producers to try to find a property they could do together. Finally, a good proposal came from Jack Rose and Mel Shavelson, the two men who had made *Room for One More*, the film about the orphans in which Grant had starred with Betsy.

The new movie would be called *Houseboat*. Again it would mark the directing debut of an established writer, this time Jack Rose. It was the story of a widower (Grant) with a bunch of children. The seven-year-old son runs away from home and meets Loren who is also running away. She takes the boy home to Grant and he asks her to stay on as a housekeeper. Naturally, they fall in love and marry in the end. But it is also a story of a man and his relationship with his children and contained many touching scenes between Grant and his kids, including a memorable one in which he is called upon to explain death.

Loren had been living for years with the Italian film producer, Carlo Ponti. He was still not divorced from his previous wife. During the filming of *Houseboat*, Loren was trying to decide whether to leave him for Grant.

Grant's relationship with Betsy had become very much a brother-sister affair. They were still close friends but now her career was starting to take off – a hit London show and several well-received movie parts. His infatuation with Loren was stronger than ever and he pressed her to consider marriage.

But, during the filming of *Houseboat*, a strange thing happened. While Loren was in Hollywood, Ponti's lawyers got him a Mexican divorce. Then they arranged his marriage to Loren by proxy, without her knowledge. Even though she never left Los Angeles, Sophia Loren was now Carlo Ponti's wife in a marriage which, while not necessarily legal in the United States, was clearly binding in her native Italy. She decided the only thing to do was to try to make a go of it with Ponti. The news devastated Grant, but he accepted her decision.

With *Houseboat* finished, and depressed about Loren, Grant decided the best medicine would be to get away from Hollywood for a while. He and Stanley Donen had already agreed that their next projects would be for their joint production company, Grandon Productions.

Grant suggested that whatever they did, it should be filmed in England. Donen agreed. Grant not only wanted to get away but he wanted to spend some time with Elsie. He asked Donen to find something they could do in England.

Donen's good friend, Norman Krasna, had written a light comedy-romance, *Kind Sir*, that was one of the hits of the current Broadway season. It was about an economics professor, played on Broadway by Charles Boyer, who meets an accomplished actress, played in New York by Mary Martin. The actress falls for the professor only to be told that although separated from his wife, he cannot get a divorce.

Later she finds he has never been married and becomes determined to make him jealous by starting a relationship with another man. It works and they end up marrying. Donen asked Krasna if he could turn it into a screenplay and change the setting from New York to London. Krasna agreed and Donen went to Warner Brothers to see if they would finance the project.

Donen found out quickly what having Cary Grant as a partner meant. 'If he wanted to make a film,' Donen remembers, 'it was not so much selling the idea as which offer to take. He had the power to get pretty much what he wanted. His biggest concern was that the movie be made correctly and that we get the best people, not only in the cast, but the crew. He had the power to pretty much name his own deal. If one studio didn't want it, another half dozen would. He could drive a very hard bargain.'

Jack Warner wanted a Cary Grant picture so badly that he offered him not only his now customary $300,000, but also guaranteed a huge production budget, gave Grandon a large share of the profits, and gave Grant a new Rolls-Royce to be kept in England.

Grant knew immediately who he wanted as his co-star. Ingrid Bergman's career had taken several strange turns since she had done *Notorious* with Grant in 1946. In 1947, she was the movie industry's top box-office attraction. Then, for a combination of reasons, mostly bad judgment in choosing roles or taking parts in films that only looked good on paper, she suffered a series of box-office failures in 1948 and 1949.

The pressure on her was heavy. She felt her only answer was to leave Hollywood for a while. She went to Italy to work with the Italian director Roberto Rossellini. The two fell in love. She had his baby.

At the time they were both married to other people. It was more than the conservative American public would accept. Bergman was raked over the coals in the press and from every pulpit and even on the floor of the US Senate. Suddenly no studio would hire her. It looked as if her American film career was at an end.

Bergman continued to make movies in Europe, several of which got limited release in the United States. Then, in 1956, 20th Century-Fox decided to take a chance. They starred her in *Anastasia*, shot in England. When released, it was an instant sensation. Hollywood let her know that all was forgiven by nominating her for the Best Actress Oscar. She won, but would not come to California to receive it. That was done for her by her friend, Cary Grant.

In accepting, Grant gave a short and simple speech: 'Dear Ingrid, wherever you are in the world, we, your friends, want to congratulate you and may you be as happy as we are for you.' She reportedly cried when she read his words.

Again, Bergman's personal life was starting to unravel. She eventually married Rossellini after both had been divorced, but now that marriage was very publicly ending.

Grant, remembering those hard times after his marriages, thought that work was the answer. He decided that he would get her as his co-star for *Indiscreet*, as *Kind Sir* had been renamed.

Donen remembers what he thought when Grant first mentioned this. 'He suggested Ingrid Bergman. I said of course but I really didn't think that we could possibly get her. It's like saying, 'Let's get Cary Grant.' That's only possible if Cary Grant wants to do the film. I just didn't think, given her personal circumstances, that Ingrid would be available. But in the end getting her was simple. He called and talked with her and then I flew over to Rome to meet with her and we talked about the film and she said yes at once.'

Grant and Donen went to London and settled in at the Connaught Hotel to begin preparing the picture. They went to the airport to meet Bergman when she arrived from Rome. A mob of reporters was there, too. They only wanted to ask about the failure of her marriage.

Years later, she recalled the scene vividly: 'I was taken into the transit lounge for a press conference, and there was Cary Grant sitting up on the table. He shouted across the heads of the journalists, "Ingrid, you think you have problems. Wait till you hear mine." That broke the ice. Everybody burst into laughter. He then held them at bay in such a nice way. "Come on, fellas, you can't ask a lady that!" "If you'll ask me that question I'll give you a better answer – I have a life twice as colourful as Ingrid's." Then we escaped and drove to the Connaught Hotel. We were all laughing. I was telling him about my problems with Roberto and he was telling me his.' With his kidding and his charm, he got her through what could have been a very tough ordeal.

Things went well on the set of *Indiscreet*. It was an enjoyable time for both Grant and Bergman. Much of the time they were shooting, Betsy was in London, first working on stage in *Next to No Time* and then preparing to co-star in a film for Richard Todd at Pinewood Studios. Even though Cary and Betsy were both in London, they didn't spend much time together. The British press had rumours flying that their marriage was at an end.

When *Indiscreet* was finished, Grant decided to have one more stab at salvaging his relationship with Betsy. He took her to spend Christmas in Monaco with Grace Kelly and her new husband, Prince Rainier. The brief holiday convinced them that while they still cared for each other, they had grown apart.

To all intents and purposes, the marriage that had begun on Christmas Day, 1949, ended at Christmas, 1957. They stayed loosely together for another four years, but it was really over. Betsy finally filed for divorce in mid-1962.

Betsy continued working in films, but also remained involved with psychotherapy. She directed a psychodrama therapy project at UCLA, and wrote a novel, *Children You're Very Young*, based on that experience.

After Monte Carlo, Grant went for a short trip to Moscow with producer Sam Spiegel. Before returning home, he visited his mother and Betsy in England.

When *To Catch a Thief* opened and turned out to be so popular, Hitchcock and Grant had promised each other they would do another film together. The director was determined that this would be a film started from scratch and built completely around the character 'Cary Grant'.

That same Christmas of 1957, Alfred Hitchcock was checking into a Miami hotel. He was due to leave the next morning for Jamaica where he and his family were going to spend the holidays. Waiting for him at the hotel were the first 70 pages of a script he had commissioned several months before from writer Ernest Lehman. Lehman's working title for the film was 'In a Northwesterly Direction'. Hitchcock called it alternatively 'Breathless' or simply, 'my Cary Grant film'.

When he hired Lehman, he explained that he wanted a plot to feature a man to whom terrible things happen, but who, through it all, remains in perfect control. He wanted the plot to develop through a series of chases. He was not sure who the hero was, or why he was being chased, he would leave that up to Lehman. But he reminded Lehman that the character was to be Cary Grant. As much as he meant Cary Grant the man, he also meant the screen personality – suave, sophisticated, charming.

Lehman had a lot of trouble getting started. A couple of times he simply wanted to give up. Finally, though, he began to see the action line more definitely, and things began to flow. When he read the first 70 pages, Hitchcock thought Lehman was right on target, it was exactly what he wanted.

Lehman told Hitchcock that it might take until April to finish the script. That didn't worry Hitchcock. He had just committed himself to directing several episodes of his 'Alfred Hitchcock Presents' television series, and had other projects in view.

He also knew that Grant would not mind a little time off. He thought he would be ready to start late in May or early in June. It took longer than that. Hitchcock ran into several problems, and cameras did not roll until August 27, 1958.

One problem Hitchcock had was Jimmy Stewart. Stewart really wanted to do the role. As the script had evolved, Stewart was aware of it. He had begged Hitchcock for a copy. He said he would hold up all projects until it was finished. 'I didn't want to come right out and tell him that I wanted Grant for the role,' Hitchcock said later. 'I told him simply that there wasn't much on paper yet. Then when he called me to say he had to report to Columbia for *Bell, Book and Candle*, I was of course very relieved.'

Another problem was casting the female lead. In *North by Northwest*, as the movie was finally called, Grant is mistaken for a spy by a secret agent played by James Mason. The real counter-agent who has infiltrated Mason's group of spies has to save Grant without revealing that she's a spy herself.

MGM insisted that Cyd Charisse play the counter-agent. Hitchcock demanded Eva Marie Saint, another of his cool blondes with a soul on fire. The fight went on for some time. Finally, with Grant's backing, the studio accepted Saint.

The final problem was what caused most of the delay. The federal government was refusing to allow the film's climactic scenes to be shot atop Mount Rushmore. Hitchcock begged and pleaded and pulled every string he could think of. Nothing worked.

Finally, he announced he would simply recreate the mountain-top with the four presidents' heads in a Hollywood soundstage and shoot it there. 'No, you won't,' said the Interior Department. Mount Rushmore, they said, was a national monument which could not in any way be reproduced without their approval.

After weeks of negotiations, a compromise was reached. Hitchcock could reproduce portions of the presidents' heads and the ending could be shot on a sound-stage if Hitchcock could just find the right camera angles. He could and he did. Those last scenes are some of Hollywood's best ever.

The delay didn't bother Grant. His deal with MGM for this movie gave him a fee of $450,000 plus ten per cent of the gross profits in excess of $8 million. On top of that, he was to get a penalty bonus of $5,000 per day for every day over seven weeks that filming took. By the time filming started, he was already a week into the penalty period. Shooting took nine weeks. The penalty came to $315,000 in his pocket, along with the original $450,000. Also, while he was waiting for *North by Northwest* to begin, *Indiscreet* opened in mid-May to rave reviews and box-office success. He was feeling just fine.

After several drafts, *North by Northwest* came to be a story of a combination of mistaken identity, political intrigue and sexual blackmail. Grant, as an innocent business executive, is mistaken for a secret agent by a group of spies. He is kidnapped, he escapes and in the process a man is killed. He is blamed for the death and now has to run from both the spies and the police. Throughout it all, he doesn't understand what is happening to him or why.

It became the last role in which Grant stretched himself as an actor. In the public mind, *North by Northwest*'s Roger Thornhill would become one of the roles most closely identified with Cary Grant.

If one were asked which picture earned Cary Grant the most money in his career, major films like *An Affair to Remember* or *To Catch a Thief* or *North by Northwest* would come to mind. In fact, his largest single earnings came from *Operation Petticoat*, which he began filming immediately after *North by Northwest*.

While he had been waiting for *North by Northwest* to begin, Grant had been approached by the faltering Universal Studios. Theatre owners were losing faith in them. They thought that Grant was just the person they needed to achieve a box-office hit.

The idea was for a comedy farce about a submarine commander, Grant, and his assistant, played by Tony Curtis, who bring their damaged sub into port to be repaired. Told it will take months to get the parts, the two steal everything needed to fix the ship and get back to the war.

At one point, the film was going to be made by Curtis and Jeff Chandler. But the two bickered over who would get top billing. The studio asked Curtis who he would accept as top billing over him, and he answered only Clark Gable or Cary Grant. Gable had just finished another submarine picture so that left only Grant.

Universal saw the film as its salvation and decided that they had to have Grant, no matter how much he cost. They offered him $750,000 plus a small percentage of the profits. He asked instead for 75 percent of the profits with only a very small guarantee. The studio badly needed a winner so they said yes.

They toyed with the possibility of quickly shooting the film before *North by Northwest* began. But it would have been just too tight. Since the film was set in the tropics of the South Pacific, they needed warm weather to shoot in. They decided to wait until the following summer, planning to have the film completed in September so that it would be released for Christmas, 1959.

Shortly after *North by Northwest* was completed, *Houseboat* opened. The reviews were nearly ecstatic. The *Hollywood Reporter* said, 'Grant's performance is just about flawless.' Another critic wrote, '*Houseboat* is the zaniest of comedies and at the same time it is a real romance. It also has in it, beautifully enunciated by Cary Grant, an essay on life and death. Mr Grant, as you know, is just about the world's smoothest, most worldly comedian. That's what he is here, but he does get in that beautiful, serious moment.'

Then, just as filming on *Operation Petticoat* began, *North by Northwest*, which had been delayed a considerable time in editing, had its long-awaited opening. Advance word in Hollywood was that it was going to be a major hit, and no one could wait to see it. Neither the critics nor the public were disappointed.

Reviewers called *North by Northwest* both Grant's and Hitchcock's best work. One wrote, 'Hitchcock and Grant are by far two of Hollywood's slickest operators. This film shows when they are together, and at the top of their game, they are unbeatable.' Another said, '*North by Northwest* is much the best Hitchcock has come along with in years. Cary Grant is just about perfect.' It went on to become the year's top grossing film.

Finally, to put a topper on what was probably Cary Grant's best year ever, *Operation Petticoat* opened at Christmas. The queues at the box office circled the block. Surprisingly, at least to Grant who didn't think the role was very demanding, it also garnered him some of his best reviews ever. *Variety* commented, 'Cary Grant is a living lesson in getting laughs without lines. In this film, most of the gags play off him. It is his reaction, always underplayed, that creates or releases the humour.'

The *Hollywood Reporter* said, 'Though he gets many laughs, Cary Grant plays an essentially straight role and theatrical pros will recognize it as one of the trickiest acting jobs of his long and brilliant career. Throughout every inch of it, he makes you feel he is a dedicated captain determined to get his ship back to sea. He makes all that follows funny instead of silly.'

Grant had not found the role demanding because he had learned to play his role so well that it had become his real self. Grant was so perfect – witty, handsome, charming, sophisticated, warm – that his fans might have come to dislike him for that very perfection. But he had one more quality that put him in movie-goers' hearts forever: he could poke fun at himself. He never took himself too seriously.

Operation Petticoat went on to earn Grant almost $4 million. He was once again among the biggest box-office attractions. As 1959 drew to a close, he was back at the very top.

10

A LIFELONG DREAM FULFILLED

THE PRODUCTION TEAM OF Cary Grant and Stanley Donen had been very pleased with the crew and the facilities when they had filmed *Indiscreet* in London. They decided to return there for their next project, *The Grass is Greener*.

They had bought the film rights to this after it had been a hit on the London stage. It had all the elements of a perfect Cary Grant movie. In the story, Victor, the Earl of Rhyall, and his wife, Lady Hilary, live in a castle. They run short of funds and are forced to open their stately home to tourists to help make ends meet. One day, a handsome tourist arrives and falls in love with Lady Hilary. Victor, in order to make his now sought-after wife jealous, pretends to have an affair with a beautiful family friend. It doesn't work. The earl and the tourist become bitter rivals, and end up fighting a farcical duel. No one gets seriously hurt, but it makes Hilary realize how much she really loves her husband. The tourist ends up going off with the family friend. It was a fun comedy in an elegant setting, filled with stylish women. In other words, it was pure Cary Grant.

Originally, Grant and Donen had wanted Rex Harrison to play one of the male leads and his wife, Kay Kendall, to play Hilary. Deborah Kerr was to play the second female lead. Those plans were scuttled by a real tragedy. Kay Kendall, just 33 years old, married for a short two years to Rex Harrison, died of leukaemia.

On *The Grass is Greener*, Deborah Kerr took over the role of Lady Hilary and Jean Simmons signed on as the family friend.

Cary Grant was to play Victor and Robert Mitchum was persuaded to play Charles, the interloper.

Because of Mitchum, the part of Charles was altered: instead of being a tourist he was a Texas millionaire who has come to England to learn how to live like a proper rich man.

Before leaving for London, Grant had tried to persuade Betsy to come with him. She didn't want to. He renewed the invitation once he arrived, and eventually she joined him. This led the British press and the Hollywood gossip columnists to write headlines that a reconciliation was in progress. When in turn she left before filming was completed, the headlines said that they had split up again. The reporters didn't know what to write when Grant and Betsy appeared hand in hand for the first Hollywood screening of the picture; and when he threw a large birthday party for her a week later.

The fact of the matter was that the two were still close friends. None of their comings and goings meant anything more than that. Betsy admitted, 'We have actually spent more time together recently since separating than we did before.'

The Grass is Greener broke Grant's string of box-office hits. It was not a success. Radio City had planned to run it as its Christmas show but backed off after seeing an early cut. The final cut was better, but it still opened to dreadful reviews.

The *Hollywood Reporter* called it 'the year's most disappointing film'. Most of the critics laid the blame on a poor script and poor on-screen chemistry between the actors. That was partly true. Deborah Kerr and Cary Grant had worked together before and had an easy relationship. Neither of them had ever worked with Jean Simmons or Robert Mitchum. It was a little like trying to bring two new members into a family. It turned out to be difficult, and the so-so result showed up on the screen.

Needless to say, the movie was a disaster at the box office.

As poorly as *The Grass is Greener* turned out, Grant was still anxious to get back to work. By now he was not interested in experimenting. Jack Warner offered him the lead in *The Music Man* but he told the producer that he was not interested in a musical. Besides, he was sure that there was no way he could do the role as well as Robert Preston had done it on Broadway.

Warner then offered him the lead in *My Fair Lady*. He wanted Grant so much that he offered $1 million plus a percentage of the profits. Again, Grant said no. As he saw it, he would either be compared to Rex Harrison, who had done it on stage, and he didn't think he could play the role as well; or he would be seen as imitating Harrison, which would not be good for either of them.

Donen offered Grant the role of the devil in *Damn Yankees*. He declined. As Donen remembers it: 'I begged and pleaded and told him how well I thought he would do with the role. But he just said no. I guess that he just didn't see himself as a devil.'

He was looking for something in the tried and true 'Cary Grant' formula. Soon after he got back to California from London, Robert Arthur brought him a script that had been written especially with Cary Grant in mind by Stanley Shapiro. Arthur had produced and Shapiro had written *Operation Petticoat*.

The movie, to be directed by Delbert Mann, was *That Touch of Mink*. It was the story of a wealthy bachelor who meets a small-town girl in New York. After an on-going, off-again relationship, they get married.

He agreed to do it. The story line was so typically 'Cary Grant' and so close to another film that Mann had directed and Shapiro had written, *Lover Come Back*, that one critic said, 'In *Lover Come Back*, the Cary Grant role was played by Rock Hudson. In *That Touch of Mink*, the Cary Grant role is played by Cary Grant. When it comes to playing Cary Grant, nobody can beat Cary Grant. Go see for yourself.'

For his co-star, Grant wanted Doris Day. It would be the only time the two would ever work together. Marty Melcher, Day's second husband and manager, demanded that she receive $750,000 for the role. Grant, still among the smartest businessmen in Hollywood, agreed to take only $600,000 but added a share of the profits. At the time, it raised a lot of eyebrows that Doris Day was being paid 'more' than Grant.

The film was a huge business. It was the first picture in history to earn more than a million dollars in a single cinema

(Radio City Music Hall). Eventually, Cary Grant earned almost as much from this movie as the $4 million he had from his 75 per cent interest in *Operation Petticoat*. The cast of *That Touch of Mink* also included Gig Young, Audrey Meadows and John Astin. Astin is memorable in the film as a creep with designs on poor Doris.

This movie proved that when Cary Grant took a 'Cary Grant' role, he was still the biggest box-office draw in the world. However, more than one critic commented that he had been playing Cary Grant for so long, it looked as if he was getting bored with the whole thing. Those words would prove to be very perceptive.

Happy with the success of *That Touch of Mink*, Grant set out to make his fourth film with Stanley Donen for their joint production company. He wanted to stick with successful formulas, but he also wanted a break from purely frivolous comedies. It took the two men only a few moments to decide that what they should do was a Hitchcock-type thriller, although without Hitchcock.

Charade was based on a short story by Peter Stone about a woman who comes home from a trip to find her house ransacked and her husband dead. A man whom she had met on her trip (Grant) offers to help her discover who killed her husband. They learn that the husband had hidden away a fortune before he died. They develop a list of possible murderers. Then, one by one, the suspects themselves are killed, until in the end, Grant narrowly manages to save the heroine from the grips of the murderer. The suspects were played by such wonderful actors as James Coburn, George Kennedy and Ned Glass. Amiable Walter Matthau turned evil as the murderer.

The big question was who to cast as the heroine. When Grant had turned down Jack Warner's very public offer of the lead in *My Fair Lady*, some of the Hollywood press had tried to say it was because he didn't want to work with Audrey Hepburn.

Nothing could have been further from the truth. Grant had turned down the part because he didn't think he could play it as well as Rex Harrison. He was unhappy about the stories that he was not interested in playing opposite Audrey Hepburn. When Stanley Donen, who had directed her previously, suggested her as perfect for the role of Reggie Lambert in *Charade*, Grant immediately agreed.

Charade was filmed entirely on location in Paris. Grant, the businessman, wanted it finished and ready to play Radio City for Christmas. This meant a tight shooting schedule. With an excellent script and firm direction by Donen, things moved both rapidly and smoothly. Although Grant had never worked with Audrey Hepburn before, they developed a quick rapport.

As Donen remembers: 'Except for that first film with Jayne Mansfield, where none of us knew each other very well, this was the first time I had worked with Cary where he had not worked with the leading lady before. With both Ingrid (Bergman) and Deborah (Kerr) he already had long-established relationships of trust and I was the new person in the group, the outsider. Here Audrey had worked with me before and we had the relationship and they both started out using me as their common bridge. But they are both absolute professionals and quickly developed a relationship and things went very well. It was as if they had worked together many times before.'

One of *Charade*'s most memorable lines and one of its most famous exchanges were ad-libbed, a sure sign that Grant and his new co-star were on the same wavelength. The line was an afterthought added by Hepburn. She was inviting Grant into her apartment. She said to him: 'Why don't you come in?' She added, 'I don't bite' – pause – 'unless it's called for.' In another scene, Hepburn was weeping copiously on Grant's shoulder. Glancing up at him, she suddenly ad libbed: 'Look, I'm getting your suit all wet.' His instant reply was, 'Don't worry, it's drip-dry.'

The film opened on schedule. Critics called it 'an absolute delight'. Of Grant himself, *Look* magazine said, 'He is still tall, dark, handsome, charming, lovable, considerate, dependable, an athletic day and night dream man who lurks deep in most women's fantasies.' It was his twenty-fifth film in Radio City and broke even the existing first-week box-office record as more than $175,000 poured through the ticket windows.

Once again Cary Grant took millions to the bank. After 30 years and 70 films, he was still on top.

Grant had come to enjoy co-producing his films with Stanley Donen. Now he thought he would go one step further. He would produce his next film by himself.

Peter Stone, who had written *Charade*, had given him another script to consider. He took it to Universal Studios where they were still grateful to him for helping to save them with *Operation Petticoat*. They approved the Stone script at once. All they had to do was to read how much money *Charade* was raking in and they would have accepted just about anything from Cary Grant so long as he would star in it. Universal even gave him the same deal terms as those for *Operation Petticoat*, his usual guarantee plus 75 percent of the profits.

The movie was *Father Goose*, and it was about as far away from the 'Cary Grant' formula as you could get. Instead of an impeccably dressed, debonair sex symbol, the film featured Grant as a heavy-drinking, slovenly eccentric hermit on a small South Pacific island, serving as a look-out for the army during the war. Grant himself described the role as 'an unshaven old grey-haired sot in sloppy denims'. Or, as he told The *New York Times*, 'I have often played the part of a spiritual bum. But this is the first time I have looked like one.'

One day the old look-out goes to a nearby island and discovers a marooned young teacher and her seven small charges, all girls. He brings them back to his island where they take over his life, pour away his booze and try to domesticate him. He naturally falls in love with the teacher and she with him. In the end, to make everything legal in the eyes of the children, he and the teacher are married by military radio.

Who to ask to co-star? He originally wanted Audrey Hepburn, but she was unavailable. He turned instead to Leslie Caron, whose Hollywood career was having its ups and downs. She was now on an upswing after her Oscar-nominated role in *The L-Shaped Room*.

Being both a star and producer was harder than Grant had anticipated. He had picked David Miller to direct, but the two did not get along, and Miller was replaced with Ralph Nelson.

Nelson had just directed the award-winning *Requiem for a Heavyweight* on television. When the producing duties became too much, Grant went to Robert Arthur and asked him to take over those day-to-day jobs.

Father Goose opened at Radio City for Christmas, 1964. It was the fifth Cary Grant film in the last six years to play the Music Hall at Christmas, its most important season.

The movie's charm was that everyone knew that Grant was simply play-acting being an old man. No one could think of him as old. Said one reviewer, 'Grant makes a strong effort, partly successful, to subdue his usual sleek self in the whiskery curmudgeon; even when the old gloss shines through, he is still a very skilful performer.'

The film itself got only mixed reviews. 'Charming' was a word used by many of the critics. But despite this, people crowded into the cinemas to see it. In its first week at Radio City, *Father Goose* took in $210,380, breaking the cinema's previous one-week record for *Charade* by more than $30,000.

Meanwhile, off the screen, Grant had been dating a young actress he had first seen in a television show.

Dyan Cannon was born Samille Diane Friesen in Tacoma, Washington, in 1939. Her father was an insurance broker. Her performing career began with singing at a Seattle synagogue. She came to Hollywood at 17 to seek her fame and fortune. By the time Grant saw her on television, she was 25, had played many television parts and had appeared in the road companies of Broadway shows.

When he had first tried to date her, Dyan played hard to get. Before long, though, she was enchanted with all the attention from such a major star. In keeping with Grant's style, it was a kind of off-again, on-again quiet relationship. She would go over to his house to watch television. They would have small dinners with close friends. Often they would not see each other for weeks or even months at a time while he was on location or she was on the road in a play.

By early 1964, the relationship was getting more serious. Dyan was touring in *How to Succeed in Business* but she would fly to California to be with Grant every weekend. In April of that year, she left the cast to be with him full-time. They often discussed marriage, at first not too seriously, but then more and more so. Dyan was willing, but Grant went back and forth. With three failed marriages, all three of which he blamed himself for, he was wary.

Grant continued to waver during the filming of *Father Goose* and through its opening at Radio City. He had taken Dyan to England to spend Christmas with his mother, now 88. During this visit he persuaded Elsie to move from her house into the Chesterfield Nursing Home in nearby Clifton. Elsie and Dyan had liked each other immediately and the visit went very well.

For years, Cary Grant had wanted a child. Many of his movies featured young children and he would often confide to his friends how much he wanted to be a father. He had been happiest during the time he was stepfather to Barbara Hutton's son, Lance. Betsy could never decide whether she wanted a child, and by the time she did, she and Grant had drifted apart.

Dyan Cannon wanted children. What's more, she wanted Cary Grant to be the father of her children. That made up his mind. In the spring of 1965, he decided to marry Dyan. The wedding was a private ceremony in Las Vegas in July, 1965. She was 26, he was 61. Fan magazine and gossip columnists went wild. Dyan retired from show business.

Immediately after the wedding, the couple left for England to see Elsie, who was delighted. The press made their visit hectic. One night they had to climb out of a back window of the Royal Hotel in Bristol where they were staying to escape the clamouring reporters and photographers.

They had only been back in California a few weeks when Dyan became pregnant. One newspaper headline screamed: 'CARY'S FOURTH EXPECTS FIRST'. They were both very pleased. Cary Grant was about to become a father for the first time at the age of 61.

The next few months were among the happiest in Cary Grant's life. He studied childbirth and parenthood. He was also busy planning his next movie. It was to be shot in Japan with the 1964 Olympics as a background. The movie was to be a remake of a 1943 comedy hit, *The More the Merrier*, which had been nominated for Best Picture that year and had won an Oscar for Charles Coburn.

The remake, called *Walk, Don't Run*, was the story of a British businessman who unexpectedly finds himself in Tokyo during the Olympics without a hotel room. The only place where he might be able to stay is in the apartment of a young woman he meets shortly after his arrival. He must get her to agree to take him in. None of his former leading ladies was interested in the film. His co-star ended up being Samantha Eggar, a young British actress, who, as it happened, was a close friend of Dyan's. This was the first time since 1932, in *Blonde Venus*, that Cary Grant didn't get the girl in the end. Eggar's love interest is played by Jim Hutton, a tall young American actor who was starting to make a name for himself.*

Not being the romantic interest was a radical departure for Cary Grant. He declared, 'My days as a leading man are over.' In a frank interview, he said, 'Movie audiences just don't want to see older men making love to younger women. And to many in the audience I am an old man.'

If he was suddenly thinking of himself as an 'old man', he was an old man that was about to become a father for the first time. The shooting schedule had been planned in such a way that Grant would be back in Hollywood well before the anticipated birth. Hardly had he stepped off the plane, though, than Dyan went into labour. On February 26, 1966, Jennifer Grant was born two months premature and weighing barely five pounds.

Of the baby's delivery, Grant said, 'Dyan did all the work, I did all the worrying. It's the one thing I am good at.' Although premature, Jennifer was a healthy baby and grew quickly. Grant doted on her. 'She's probably the only completely perfect baby in the world,' he would tell friends.

Grant wanted his mother to see Jennifer, so in July he, Dyan and Jennifer embarked on a four-month trip to Europe. Elsie Leach, still quick-minded, loved her new granddaughter.

---

* Jim Hutton died tragically in an accident in 1979 at the early age of 46. His son, Timothy Hutton, is one of the hottest young stars of the 80s.

Unfortunately, the happiness was not to last. Cary and Dyan were having trouble. By the time they got back to California in October, they realized that the marriage wasn't working. Except for Jennifer, they seemed to have little or nothing in common. Grant was quiet and obsessively private. Dyan was outgoing and public. She thought that marriage and fatherhood would change him. If anything, it made him even more private and more of a stay-at-home.

Shortly after Christmas, Cary and Dyan separated. He was distraught. He found it intolerable to be away from his daughter. He was terrified he would lose her.

Dyan moved to New York to return to the stage. Grant followed her to stay near Jennifer. He lived with his friend, publicist Bob Taplinger.

Dyan filed for divorce. Cary begged her to come back. She refused. In the long, bitter divorce battle, she accused him of using LSD and of beating her in front of the servants. Finally, Dyan was granted her divorce. The judge, though, gave Grant liberal parental visiting rights. He and Jennifer remained close.

Grant's fourth marriage was over. But he had access to his heart's desire, his daughter. He was never anything but an adoring father.

11

'OLD CARY GRANT FINE'

CARY GRANT NEVER ACTUALLY announced his final retirement. It just sort of happened. He himself didn't seem to have planned it.

Walk, Don't Run opened to generally good reviews. He might not have got the girl, but Grant appeared as suave and debonair as ever. *Newsweek* was moved to comment, 'In one of his wonderful dissertations on ancient history, Will Cuppy posed the question of why the pyramids have not fallen down. He then supplied the answer. They have not fallen down because it is not in their nature to fall down. A pyramid could not fall down if it wanted to. The explanation applies equally well to Cary Grant, who could not be unfunny if he tried. Grant has watched the decline of Hollywood comedy first hand, and in *Walk, Don't Run*, he tried almost singlehandedly to prevent its complete downfall.'

This last film was not among the highest grossing of Cary Grant's pictures, but it did make a respectable showing. There was no outward sign that anything had changed in his career. He had been talking about retirement again, but he had 'retired' before and had come back bigger than ever. This time, he just became preoccupied with the rest of his life. He managed to retire without any formal idea of doing so.

In the months following the release of *Walk, Don't Run*, he would normally have been looking at scripts, meeting friends and studios about possible projects, even preparing his next film. But this time, Grant was so caught up in his battle with Dyan and with trying to stay close to Jennifer that movies were the furthest thing from his mind.

By the time his life was more settled, movies had simply lost their appeal. He said that he never made any conscious decision to end his career. It just happened.

He was often asked if he would make another film. For years his standard reply was, 'Yes, it's possible. It's possible I might make ten more. I just don't know.' Eventually, as the years went by, his stock answer changed to, 'That part of my life is over. I don't have the energy for it any more. I loved my work, so I had fun making movies. But now it's something that I used to do.'

Gradually, without even thinking about it, at least not at first, he just turned his back on Hollywood and walked away. Why? Perhaps he did not like what he saw on the screen in *Walk, Don't Run* in 1966. Perhaps it was because in that film, someone else, not he, got the girl. After it was over, he laughed about it, saying that it was only natural given his advancing years. But behind the laughter, he seemed to be serious.

Cary Grant had stopped being 'Cary Grant', or at least was about to do so. He knew it, and more than likely, didn't want to come up with someone new. He had never been much of a character actor after all.

It's important to remember that this was 15 years before *On Golden Pond*, the breakthrough movie that allowed the wonderful Katharine Hepburn and Henry Fonda to play good, meaty roles despite their ages. The 1960s and 1970s didn't provide much for older actors. By the time Hollywood started to remedy this in the mid-1980s, Grant had completely lost interest in acting.

His friend and partner, Stanley Donen, who was close to Grant in the last years of his active film career, says he was saddened but not particularly surprised at the decision. 'I was not surprised when he retired. He had been saying he was going to do it for a long time. He didn't want to play old men on the screen. Of course he wasn't (an old man), isn't even today, despite his age. He just didn't want to turn himself into a caricature of himself. And he had the courage to do it, to simply walk away. So many times you see actors and actresses just trying to hang on for one more film and then one more. He didn't. He had the class to simply quit when he thought it was time.'

His long-time friend and collaborator, the director Howard

Hawks, saw it coming, too. In 1963, while Grant was still filming *Charade*, Hawks was trying to persuade him to do another film. 'I had this terrific script,' Hawks remembered, '*Man's Favourite Sport*. He'd have been great in it. He just said, "I'm not going to play with three young girls." He just didn't want to make a picture with a young girl. We eventually made the film with Rock Hudson and it was a pretty good film. Rock worked hard but he was not a comedian. Cary would have been so much better.'*

In later years, Grant himself tried to explain his decision by using an analogy he came to call 'A Streetcar Named Aspire'.

'Well, in Hollywood we have this strange thing that I call "A Streetcar Named Aspire". The thing about this particular streetcar is that it is only so big, and there are only so many seats on it. When somebody new gets on somebody else has to get off. When I got on, for example, Warner Baxter had to get off. When Tyrone Power got on, Ronald Colman had to get off. And when Gregory Peck got on someone else had to get off. Of course some got off more slowly than others and some even ran around to the front and got on again as character actors. Adolphe Menjou was a good example of that. And a few never got off at all, like Clark Gable, and Gary Cooper who never got off either. He just stuck his long legs out into the aisle and stayed there.'

After *Walk, Don't Run*, it was clear to him if to no one else that it was time to get off. It would not do for 'Cary Grant' to get back on board as a character actor.

One of Grant's biographers, Richard Schickel, expressed it this way in his book, *Cary Grant: A Celebration*. 'Having created "Cary Grant" out of a cloth as whole as that out of which Walt Disney created Mickey Mouse, he felt entirely free to dispense with him, erase him as it were. And in much the same manner that he had created him, that is to say in a subtle and seemly and slightly mysterious manner, without shock to his or to anyone else's nervous system, without regrets and without undignified appeals to nostalgic sentiment.'

* *Hawks on Hawks* by Joseph McBride (University of California Press, 1982).

Although out of show business, Cary Grant still had a great deal that he wanted to do. He was an active man and had no intention of becoming less active. He was wealthy and a lot of his time was devoted to managing his business interests. Cary Grant the actor was about to become Cary Grant the full-time businessman.

Through his New York friend, Bob Taplinger, Grant had been introduced to George Barrie. Barrie was a former musician who had founded the very successful cosmetics firm, Rayette-Fabergé. Almost immediately after his divorce from Dyan, Barrie flew Grant back to New York on his private jet. During the trip, the two men worked out a deal that was to take Hollywood by surprise. Barrie knew that Grant's image of class and style was just what his company needed. Grant joined Fabergé's board of directors and became a consultant to and a spokesman for the company. He travelled around the world for Fabergé. When the announcement was made that Grant had joined them, the company's stock rose a full two points.

Not long after that, he became a member of the board of directors of MGM. To mark his tenth year on that board and for his eightieth birthday, MGM renamed its studio theatre the Cary Grant Theatre. He also became a board member of Hollywood Park race-track, the Princess Grace Foundation and the Kennedy Center in Washington, D.C.

For a while, he moved his centre of operations to New York, living in a large apartment in the Warwick Hotel on east 54th Street. Then he decided that he wanted to have a better home for Jennifer when she was with him. He bought a new house on five acres of land in Beverly Hills. He also kept the house in Palm Springs and added a weekend house in Malibu and a vacation home in the Bahamas.

He and Dyan became somewhat friendlier again. He helped her get some movie roles, and she agreed to increase his visiting rights with Jennifer. He now saw his daughter every other weekend and at least once a week. He never missed a visiting day. No matter where in the world he was, he always flew back to California for his day or weekend with Jennifer.

On January 22, 1973, just two weeks short of her 96th birthday, Elsie Leach died in a nursing home in Clifton. She insisted she was only 93. In her final years, she had been delighted to have a grandchild at last. She always kept a picture of Jennifer nearby. Said Grant, 'She died peacefully after having rung for her tea. That's a nice way to die. I often wonder how I'm going to do it. You don't want to embarrass your friends.'

Eventually, Cary Grant got rid of many of his ties to show business. His contracts for many of his later movies gave him ownership of the negatives after a period of five to eight years after their release. In 1975, he owned all the rights to his last ten pictures except for the Hitchcock films. In one deal, he now sold them all for a total of more than $2 million. When home video cassettes became so popular, he was asked if he thought he'd been short-sighted. 'No,' was his reply, 'it was time.'

For years after he retired, film offers continued to arrive almost weekly. He dismissed them all immediately, even though many would have allowed him to name his own price. Warren Beatty offered him $1 million to make a cameo appearance in *Heaven Can Wait*. Joe Mankiewicz wanted him to star in the film version of the hit play, *Sleuth*. Grant turned it down and the part went to Laurence Olivier. His friend George Barrie tried to persuade him to make a comeback in a film that Barrie had acquired called *A Touch of Class*. He said no, telling Barrie. 'Ten years ago I would have made it in a second, but not now.' That role went to George Segal.

The offers continued to come. One day a producer called with an extraordinary offer: he would give Grant $2 million plus almost all the profits to star in a film with the improbable name of *One Thousand Cups of Crazy German Coffee*. Grant thanked him politely, but said no, he really was retired. When he hung up, he had a huge laugh. Although this producer who now owned the script had no idea, Grant had owned it years before and would have made the film then if he had had the time.

Grant also worked at becoming a regular at the LA Dodger baseball games.

He used to recall the first baseball game he ever saw. It was in New Orleans while he was on tour with the Penders in 1920. The boys in the troupe did not have much money, but they wanted to see the games. They made a deal with the ball club. They would mention the team every night in their act in exchange for free tickets. Grant's love of baseball grew over the years.

On one of his trips to England for Fabergé, Cary Grant met a young hotel publicist, Barbara Harris. Barbara was 25. She had been born and brought up in Tanzania, where her father had been a British Army officer. She admitted later that while she knew who he was when she first met him, growing up as she had in Africa, she had not seen many of his films.

He and Barbara had a courtship that lasted several years, back and forth across the Atlantic. In 1979, Barbara finally agreed to move to California and live with him. Early in 1981, when he was 77, he asked Jennifer if she minded him marrying Barbara. When his daughter encouraged him to do so, he married for the fifth time. It was a very private ceremony on the terrace of his Beverly Hills home in April of that year. The only witnesses were Jennifer and Grant's long-time butler.

They both kept the marriage secret, but a few weeks later they attended a twenty-fifth wedding anniversary party for Prince Rainier and Princess Grace (Kelly) at the Palm Springs home of Frank Sinatra. It was a very small gathering; everyone there had known each other for years. To this small group of friends, the new Mr and Mrs Cary Grant admitted their secret. Within days, it was in all the papers. Grant was disappointed. 'They're all old chums,' he said. 'I thought they'd keep our secret.'

In 1984, Cary Grant turned 80. To his many fans it was a milestone to be celebrated. Not to him. He said he would simply spend the day at home with Barbara and Jennifer and a few friends might drop over for the evening. He told reporters, 'I'm glad I made it, but there isn't any reason for a special celebration. I'm going to duck everyone and keep a low profile.'

The world couldn't leave it at that. There was an outpouring of affection from fans everywhere and from the media. A lot was made of how young he continued to look. 'We do not know the secrets,' wrote one columnist. 'Every generation or so he takes unto himself a young wife. Perhaps that is what does it. Some men seek out lost youth and indulge second childhoods with illicit drugs, with the purchase of sports cars, with face-lifts and dancing lessons. Cary Grant needs none of these things. Young women, old tweeds and whatever mysterious flame that burns within, these seem enough to keep him young. Cary Grant 80? Ridiculous. You might as well try to convince Virginia there is no Santa Claus.'

Happy with his new wife and his solid relationship with Jennifer, Grant started to meet his public again with his 'Evenings with Cary Grant'.

These were adoring audiences. Most had paid good money to come and hear him talk and most would have gladly stood in long queues at the box office to see him in films once again. The most often asked question was 'Why, oh why, did he retire?' His usual answer was the 'Streetcar Named Aspire' analogy. But one night he answered that question more simply, and possibly more from the heart. Reported in *Parade* magazine on September 22, 1985, his reply ran:

'I'd prefer to be younger and know what I know today and be able to apply it to life in every aspect. But I am happy. I get up every morning and go to bed every night, and occupy myself as best I can in between. I do what I want when I want. Once, in St Louis, I met a fellow who ran a whorehouse because it made him happy. Well, I do what makes me happy.'

As he made these appearances, it was almost as if he remembered his famous old line, 'Everybody wants to be Cary Grant. I want to be Cary Grant.' Even though he would find himself standing in front of packed houses, he always seemed amazed that people were still interested in him and his films. He did the Evenings, it seems, so that he could continue to answer, 'OLD CARY GRANT FINE'. Perhaps he remembered a line he once delivered to Ginger Rogers in *Monkey Business*, 'You're only old when you forget you're young.'

As long as we can see his movies, Cary Grant will always be young to his devoted fans.

INDEX

Italicised entries are films unless otherwise indicated